SHE LOOKS JUST LIKE YOU

She Looks Just Like You

A Memoir of
(Nonbiological Lesbian)
Motherhood

Amie Klempnauer Miller

Beacon Press
BOSTON

BEACON PRESS
25 Beacon Street
Boston, Massachusetts 02108-2892
www.beacon.org

Beacon Press books
are published under the auspices of
the Unitarian Universalist Association of Congregations.

26 25 24 23   8 7 6 5

This book is printed on acid-free paper that meets the uncoated paper ANSI/NISO specifications for permanence as revised in 1992.

Portions of this book, in slightly different versions, have been previously published as "Babymaking," Salon.com, August 11, 2004; "New Day, Neurosis," *Brain, Child* (Winter 2005); "Not a Mommy, Yet Not a Dad," *Brain, Child* (Winter 2006); and "Watching," in *Confessions of the Other Mother: Nonbiological Lesbian Moms Tell All!* ed. Harlyn Aizley (Boston: Beacon Press, 2006).

The names of some people in the text have been changed, as have the identification numbers of all sperm donors mentioned.

Text composition by Wilsted & Taylor Publishing Services, Oakland, CA

"Love Will Guide Us" © 1985 Sally Rogers, Thrushwood Press Publishing. Used by permission of Sally Rogers, Thrushwood Press Publishing.

Library of Congress Cataloging-in-Publication Data

Miller, Amie Klempnauer
  She looks just like you : a memoir of (nonbiological lesbian) motherhood / Amie Klempnauer Miller.
    p. cm.
  ISBN 978-0-8070-0151-6 (paperback : alk. paper) 1. Miller, Amie Klempnauer. 2. Nonbiological mothers — United States — Biography. 3. Lesbian mothers — United States — Biography. 4. Gender identity — United States. I. Title.
  HQ75.53.M65 2010
  306.874'3086640973 — dc22   2009029937

To Jane, to Hannah

CONTENTS

ONE

Babymaking

[1]

JANE AND I ARE STANDING in our very pink bathroom, staring at the two very blue lines on the pregnancy test stick in Jane's hand. Jane took the test precisely when she wasn't supposed to: in the evening, after dinner, immediately after drinking a large glass of lemonade. She is supposed to do it first thing in the morning, when her body, if it is indeed pregnant, will have had sufficient time to store up enough undiluted human chorionic gonadotropin, that telltale pregnancy hormone, to trip the test line on the stick into blue territory. But she couldn't wait, and it didn't matter. The line on her stick turned blue immediately, a bird's egg, summer sky blue that left no room for doubt. She's not only pregnant, she is decisively pregnant. After eighteen years of just the two of us, we are going to become three.

"I *knew* it," Jane says. On some level, I did too. For the past several days, she has come home from work exhausted and voracious. Either she was pregnant or she had developed a severe metabolic disorder. But even though I suspected a positive result, I am still wowed. I feel disoriented, as though the journey from one blue line to two has played out cosmically, bridging the time-space continuum. It feels like magic. Maybe it is.

Pregnancy is always hypothetical until it happens. Until this moment, pregnancy has stayed at a tantalizing, but safe, arm's length. Now it is here, in our bathroom, hugging us like an unfamiliar and overly affectionate aunt. I gape at Jane. I can scarcely believe that her body has already begun the alchemy of transforming proteins and hormones into a new body, a new person. I am stunned by the very notion that we are actually going to be mothers, not just crabby armchair observers kvetching about how children need bed-times and how kids today don't have any boundaries.

I stare at our faces in the mirror. We look the same as we did before dinner, which strikes me as odd. We should look different, I think. We should look pregnant, or at least expectant. I take the test stick from Jane's hand and study it, checking to make sure I didn't somehow hallucinate the result. They're still there: the control line and the one that mesmerizes me, the test line—our blue line, our baby.

"That's my family," Jane says, shaking her head. "Wave a little sperm at us and we get knocked up."

This is not how we thought it would happen. Two weeks ago, I went with Jane to the fertility clinic where she was inseminated. It was the same clinic where I had gone month after month for a year and a half, trying to conceive. The same magazines with the same articles about safe exercise during pregnancy and the virtues of breastfeeding lay on the end tables in the waiting room. The same nurse who had repeatedly inserted one man's sperm after another's into me now inseminated Jane. Everything, in fact, was the same ex-cept that, this time, I sat in a chair and watched as my partner lay on the exam table, her sock-covered feet lodged in the metal stirrups. In the weeks prior to the appointment, Jane had been ambivalent about whether I should come along or not.

"It's just a medical procedure," she said. She was right, in one sense. After ten or twelve inseminations of my own, the process became increasingly medicalized, even routine. I began to go to the clinic by myself, stop in for a quick insemination, and then drop by the coffee shop for a scone and some tea before heading to the office. I would call Jane to report on how it went, but there seemed little reason for her to tag along time after time. This was different, though. It was Jane's first try, and even though inseminating with donor sperm is kind of like going on a blind date chaperoned by a nurse, I wanted to be there.

"It's not like you're going in for a Pap smear," I said. "Anyway, I don't want to tell our kid that I was in a meeting at the moment of conception."

So, along I went. Jane lay on the table draped in a paper sheet, her feet pointed northwest and northeast. The nurse adjusted the light over Jane's hips, inserted the speculum into her vagina, and peered inside.

"You're looking great," the nurse said. "Lots of good mucus here. That's wonderful."

Then she looked at me and offered, "Do you want to see?"

"Uh, no," I said. That's a lesbian moment I don't need to have.

The nurse navigated the loaded catheter through Jane's cervix and into her uterus, where she deposited the sperm. She adjusted the exam table, elevating Jane's hips six inches so that gravity could help the sperm on their journey. As she left the room, she waved her fingers in the air.

"Good luck!" she said cheerily.

Jane settled in to wait the prescribed ten minutes, presumably enough time for the sperm to find their way.

"Did it hurt?" I asked her.

"Not really," she said. "A little pinching, but not bad." Insemination is a remarkably simple process, really, if also an unsentimental one. Once the nurse confirms that the number of the donor listed on the vial of sperm is, in fact, the number of the donor whose sperm we ordered, she just loads up the catheter and inserts the goods. The only real reason to do it in a doctor's office rather than at home is that the nurse can get the sperm all the way into the uterus rather than just leaving it in the vagina, thereby raising the chances that at least one sperm will find its way to the egg.

Still, I had little expectation that anything would come of this visit to the clinic. I had to try twenty times before ultimately conceding defeat, so I figured Jane would need to try at least three or four times before hitting the target. I counted out the months, estimating when she might reasonably get pregnant. It was June, so September, I figured, maybe October.

Jane rubbed her hand on her abdomen.

"Are you having cramps?" I asked quickly. I had a fair amount of cramping after my first fruitless insemination, my cranky uterus upset about the prodding of the catheter.

"Hmm? No. Just, I don't know."

As we left the building and walked into the parking lot, Jane began to cry.

"I'm going to get pregnant," she whispered. "It's really going to happen." She looked shaken and unsteady. Tears pressed out of her eyes. I took her arm in mine and we walked slowly around the perimeter of the parking lot. She seemed almost faint, as though she had just seen a ghost or, maybe, a glimpse of her future.

"I didn't know until now how much I wanted this," she said. "I just had no idea."

[II]

How do you decide to have a baby? Jane and I, because we are lesbians and fully endowed with the lesbian love of process, devoted a full ten years of conversation to it. Should we, shouldn't we, should we, shouldn't we? For years, we seemed unable to say unequivocally, "This is what we want, not that." Having a baby would lead to one path; not having a baby to another.

About six years ago, we took a "Maybe Baby" class designed for lesbians. Week after week, we sat in a big circle with thirty-one other lesbians at Chrysalis—A Center for Women. Jane and I had signed up for the class in the hope that it would help us decide whether or not to have a child. We were looking for some guidance in deciding whether to turn down the Babies "R" Us aisle of life. We wanted to hear discussion of how other couples were making their decisions—to understand if our hopes were naive, our fears excessive, or if we were listening too much to our heads and ignoring our hearts.

What we got instead was a barrage of information on how to make or acquire a baby. There were lots of handouts on the mechanics and logistics of "alternative" insemination. ("There's nothing 'artificial' about it," the instructor reminded us.) We learned about the many legal issues faced by same-sex parents. Because parental rights are largely tied to marriage and biology, the law typically recognizes only one member of a same-sex couple—the biological parent—as the legal parent of a child. If there is a breakup, the unrecognized parent can be denied the right to custody. If the legal parent dies, a child can be placed with blood relatives or even become a ward of the state. The wobbly legal status of the unrecognized parent also means that he or she may not be permitted to give consent for medical treatment, provide health insurance for the child, or in some cases, even visit that child in the hospital. A child would be ineligible for Social Security benefits if the unrecognized parent should die and would have no legal claim to an inheritance, should there be one. The reality is that the laws governing same-sex families vary from state to state and even county to county. We learned that pretty much everything was being decided on a case-by-case basis. The strength of the legal bond that could be forged between a child and a non-birth parent depended largely on where the family lived and the mood and political inclinations of the presiding judge.

We also learned about adoption and foster care. As residents of

Minnesota, we could adopt a child—well, one of us could. Like most other states, the legal ability of a same-sex couple to adopt jointly was unclear. Maybe it would work; maybe it wouldn't. The best bet, should we pursue either domestic or international adoption, would be for one of us to become the legal parent and for the other to petition the court for a second-parent adoption. Foster care was a legal possibility in Minnesota, but that did not seem like the right option for us, given our profound inexperience. Everything we learned was important and useful, but it didn't help us make a decision. Jane and I didn't need to talk about how to make or get a baby, but about why we might want to do so in the first place.

To our astonishment, we were the only women in the Maybe Baby class who fell into the "maybe" category. Everyone else had already decided to have a child; some were already trying. Their certainty was intimidating to me, not to mention mystifying. One woman even said she had known she wanted to be a mommy since she was four years old. I was incredulous. When I was four, I wanted to be an acrobat.

After the class ended, we began looking for direction from friends with infants, friends with toddlers, and friends with adolescents. They told us about the wonders of raising a child and how sometimes they just wanted to flush the kid. We got stuck in a six-month stalemate after lesbian friends who, ironically enough, had the same first name, became the moms of twins, like a Doublemint gum commercial come to life. They followed the attachment model of parenting and practiced "baby wearing"—holding the babies as close as possible to the parents' bodies for as much time as possible, over as many months as possible. For weeks, the birth mom did little but hold and nurse and hold and nurse babies.

"Oh, good Lord, no," Jane said after visiting them. "Just no."

We also looked at the lives of lesbians we know who do not have children. Some devoted themselves to gardening and political activism. They traveled, spent weekends at their cabin near the Boundary Waters, and went out when they wanted to. But some were still "deciding" on parenthood at age forty-five. Or they spent all of their time at the office. Or they had disturbingly close relationships with their pets.

Which of these futures did we want? Not the one where we dress up the cats.

Time and again, people told us that we would be good parents, but that didn't make our decision any easier. Jane and I suspected that they thought we were good parenting material because we are, to put it bluntly, boring. We have been married, effectively if not officially, for nearly two decades. We are so monogamous that we even have a hard time identifying celebrities who we think are sexy. Jane's ideal evening is snuggling down on the couch with two cats and three or four books on her lap while *Songs of the Auvergne* plays on the stereo. Meanwhile, I settle in on the other end of the couch, sip my vanilla tea and do some cross-stitching. For excitement, we play Scrabble.

With no clear reason to choose yes or no, we talked endlessly. Because Jane and I believe that it is virtually impossible to over-think a decision, we designed a retreat for ourselves during which we discussed the pros and cons of parenthood. We sat in the living room, eating banana muffins that I had baked earlier that morning, and discussed the ground rules for our retreat. We would think out of the box, we agreed. We would, not surprisingly, talk about how we felt. We agreed to try not to digress, a challenge for both of us. And, we agreed, we would let this discussion and process of decision making be whatever it is. Whatever that meant.

Then we made up a list of open-ended statements for each of us to complete:

The things I like about having a child are....
The things I don't like about having a child are....
The things that scare me about having a child are....

The things that scare me about not having a child are....
I think my partner thinks....
I think my partner feels.....

While we chewed our muffins, Jane and I wrote our answers on our respective legal pads and then shared our responses with each other. We both liked the idea of nurturing a child, of playing, and of passing something on to the next generation. We both believed that we have a lot to offer. Neither one of us liked the expense of raising a child. And we were both concerned about whether we would ever manage to fit in with other parents. To be honest, we wondered if we would even like other parents.

"What scares you most about having a child?" I asked Jane midway through the morning.

"Losing my independence," she said after a minute. "Losing my sense of self." For Jane, the grown-up version of the little girl who got an F on a paper in grade school because she refused, on principle, to write her name in the upper-right-hand corner of the page where her teacher, on principle, believed it must go, independence and sense of self have always gone hand in hand. As long as I have known her, Jane has never seemed to want the kind of independence that is averse to relationships; she has no problem with commitment. But she wants to live life on her terms, writing her name where she thinks it should go.

It would never have occurred to me not to write my name where the teacher instructed. I would have written it, neatly and carefully, in the right-hand corner and would have frowned on Jane for being disruptive. Looking at parenthood, I worried about new sets of rules, foreign to me, to which I would need to comply. I was less afraid of what I would lose than of what I might have to become. Would I have to drive an SUV? Would I know how to be nurturing enough? Would I need to become someone or something that I'm not? Could I become a mother? What if I failed?

I distrust maternal instinct, particularly my own. I am not sure what it feels like, what it means to mother instinctively. Do other women have a maternal compass guiding them? If so, mine seems to point north on some days and south on others, with a good deal of east in between. The truth is that I have never thought of myself as particularly maternal. Other people have often seen me as a little aloof, a little cold, perhaps slightly withdrawn. Granted, there are plenty of aloof and cold mothers in the world, but that's not what I want to be. Do I have the emotional generosity to mother a child? I don't know. Can I fall in love with a child? The only way I know how to find out is to try, but it strikes me as a particularly perilous experiment.

Does every woman see the possibility of parenthood through the lens of her own mother? We know what it means to mother by being mothered—or not being mothered. Books can help, of course, but the lessons of experience are deeper and stickier. My mother was a grab bag of maternalism and anti-maternalism. When my friends and I set up lemonade stands, she made batches of fresh cookies for us to sell. When my sister had a little playhouse in the backyard, my mother wrote notes from Mr. Frog and Ms. Chipmunk and stashed them in the play mailbox. A religion major in college and a frustrated minister's wife, my mother would sit in church on Sunday mornings and take notes on my father's sermon. They would discuss it afterward: sections that could have been stronger, points that came through particularly well. She turned her artistic talents into wallpaper glue and paint thinner, completely redecorating every parsonage where we ever lived. She looked forward each week to the Cleveland classical radio station's broadcast of the Metropolitan Opera, but then a few days later, she would sink into bed, snared in a net of darkness. She rode on waves of depression and spikes of fury. Neither of these emotions is on the list of what it means to be maternal, although given how common they are, perhaps they should be.

Would this be my future, too? What would it mean to become a mother myself? Would I become my mother, reversioned? Or myself, revised? Can I launch my boat on the waves of motherhood and navigate? Or will I just have to walk into the surf and be carried wherever the currents—or the riptide—might take me?

Jane and I turned to fresh sheets of paper and wrote a list of options for the future. We could opt to have a child. Or we could choose not to have a child. We could find a way to have kids in our lives part-time. We could start inseminating. We could try to adopt. We could become foster parents. We could get involved with local organizations that work with gay and lesbian youth. We could become Big Sisters. We could volunteer with Head Start. We could make a point of getting more involved with our nieces and nephews or with our friends' children. We could host an exchange student.

If we decided not to have a child, we would have more freedom. We would have more money. We could pursue different professional opportunities. We could live abroad. We could arrange our lives so that we take every summer off. We could create our own sabbatical and travel the world for a year. But would we?

If we decided not to have a child, we would never know what parenting is like. We would never know how much love or passion or fear or, for that matter, outright misery could come with it. We would never know what it is like to watch our child learn to live in the world.

But if we decided to have a child, we would—what? The question is unanswerable. We could look at the lives of friends, we could read books, we could figure out the common denominators of parenthood: changing diapers, worrying about food in and food out, joining PTAs, selling candy to coworkers, trying to survive adolescence. We knew that if we decided to have a child, our lives would transform, but we had no real idea what that might mean or if the transformation would make us happy. How do you know if a life transformed is the life desired? How do you see what is on the other side of the abyss without leaping across?

It's a mixed blessing to have to make an explicit decision about parenthood. While straight people often assume future parenthood in the same way that they might assume the certainty of a spring wedding, the default option for gay men and lesbians traditionally has been not to have children. Accidental pregnancies are not a big problem in our community. We generally have to seek out parenthood if we want it to happen. On the plus side, we are almost never harassed by eager grandparents about whether we have started "trying," wink, wink. As with adoptive parents or infertile couples, our children must be chosen and pursued. There's a certain smugness that often goes with this: we worked for our children, they didn't just happen. But the need to make a concrete decision sometimes carries the risk of getting drowned in a tidal wave of mixed emotions. And the need to involve outsiders (doctors, donors, lawyers, nurses, and in some cases, social workers, birth parents, or surrogates) encourages procrastination. Jane and I got to think about it, but we also had to think about it. That was our quandary.

We searched for a reasoned answer about parenthood, or even an instinctive one, and came up empty. We could choose this path—or not. And so, in the end, we decided to "put ourselves in the path of pregnancy." We would let the fates decide, but first, we would hand the fates a catheter and a vial of sperm.

[I I I]

We began by looking for a Man. What we ended up picking were the characteristics of a man, a semi-fictional guy, hidden behind a scrim of anonymity. We briefly considered asking a friend to contribute sperm. We had a couple of gay men in mind, both the warm, nurturing, paternal sort. We would want them involved in the life of any child we might have, we reasoned, so why not ask them to be there from the very, very beginning?

We had reason to believe that such an arrangement could work. About a block away from us lived a family that had successfully woven together a gay biological dad, two moms, and two kids. They had all committed to living in the same neighborhood until the kids were grown. They were all explicit about seeing themselves as parents and seemed happy and well adjusted. It was like a gay Brady Bunch.

But we also knew of a gay man who had donated sperm to lesbian friends and then spent years and more than $100,000 in court fighting over custody issues. And, truthfully, Jane and I knew that we are just the tiniest bit opinionated; some might even say controlling. While the idea of making cookies together as a blended family unit sounded charming, the thought of making all of our parenting decisions by committee sounded positively suffocating.

Anonymity promised a sense of privacy and a sense of safety. We would be less vulnerable, we reasoned, if there were no third person who could claim rights to the child. We would not have to face a custody battle because an anonymous donor would not know of our existence. We would not have to feel as though we had married an additional person—or worse, two.

But more than that, we wanted to ensure that we would be our child's real parents. We wanted each of us to be seen as a parent—not one of us as a parent and one of us as something else, not quite named. We knew that our parenthood would be out of the ordinary simply because our child would have two mothers. But we wanted to create a family that would be as normal as possible, even if it would be abnormal by definition. Choosing an anonymous donor made us feel that our family would be (mostly, kind of) a normal American nuclear family, with a twist. Despite the fact that the "typical" American family—with its married mother and father and its two cherubic kids—is becoming more atypical every year, it is still accepted as the norm. So long as there is a father—or even just a father figure—around somewhere, it becomes extremely challenging for most people to recognize two legitimate, full-fledged, equal mothers. In the shadow of the 'real' parents—the mother and the father—the second mother is just that: second. She is other, mom's lesbian partner, a friend. Jane and I knew that if we were going to be parents, we were damned well both going to be parents. If one of us was going down, by God, so was the other.

So, we went shopping for sperm. Or rather, I went shopping for sperm. Jane's theory of shopping—for clothes, a house, a man—is that a comparison of two is really one more than necessary. She will look at two choices, quickly select one, and be done. I, on the other hand, believe that the existence of a good choice and a better choice must mean that there is a perfect choice out there somewhere. It's my job to find it.

Anyway, it seemed only fair that I should do the shopping. We had decided that we would start with my uterus, largely because I was more willing to offer up my body to the travails of pregnancy. This was more out of ignorance than nobility. Jane has had pregnant sisters and more pregnant friends than I've had. Her view of pregnancy is unsparingly realistic, focused on swollen ankles and gradually splitting pelvises. I liked to think about the romance of it all, that whole Miracle of Life thing, so Jane kindly suggested that I go first.

Armed with a mug of tea and half a dozen chocolate chip cookies, I sat in front of the computer in our spare bedroom and pored over one online catalogue of sperm donors after another. There was the Sperm Bank of California, which touted its identity-release program, offering our future child the option to contact the donor upon turning eighteen. There was the lesbian-owned Pacific Reproductive Services in San Francisco. There was Cryogenic Laboratories, the first private sperm bank in the country, just a few miles away in Roseville, Minnesota. After several hours, I decided to focus on the Roseville sperm bank, in part because it was close to our home and I felt a sense of familiarity with, as it were, the breeding stock. I clicked on Donor #4356 and read that he is outgoing, friendly and athletic, but his family has a history of cancer. Donor #642 was raised Lutheran and is now agnostic. His mother has high blood pressure; his uncle had a stroke. Donor #574 is a six-foot college student with blond hair and hay fever who likes to work on cars, enjoys jazz music, and wants to travel to Tibet. Which one of these could be Dad?

I stared at the screen, wondering what the donors might look like and whether or not I would like them. Without knowing exactly what to look for, I adhered to a few guidelines of my own devising: Don't take anyone who says he likes to laugh at his own jokes. Avoid donors described by the sperm bank's intake worker as "unique." To be honest, I wanted Mr. Right. I was drawn to donors who had completed higher education degrees or at least had aspirations to do so. I went for the guys with the medium builds—not too tall, too short, or too fat. I eliminated anyone with a close family history of cancer, chemical abuse, diabetes, or, God forbid, multiple births. I made sweeping judgments based on the small amount of personal description provided. This donor likes cars; I don't. That donor's not very athletic; neither am I, but is he just lazy?

Staring at the monitor, I tried to imagine what is essentially unimaginable: what a baby will be like before it is even conceived. I wanted to find a donor who could be a genetic proxy for Jane, because what we really wanted, truth be told, was to make a baby together. I wanted this anonymous man to be a silent partner, to transmit the qualities Jane would give if we could make a baby ourselves. I looked for intelligence: Jane is a university administrator with a Ph.D. who reads biographies of Cicero for fun. I looked for someone who seemed nurturing to match her strong maternal bent and fondness for small animals. I looked for someone musical because she sings. I looked for someone opinionated because she is that, too. At last, I found a donor who had a doctorate, sang in a choir, and—the clincher—was a cat lover. That was my boy, my lesbian stand-in.

I had already preregistered with the sperm bank, signing on the dotted line to confirm my understanding that the donor is now and shall remain anonymous, that I cannot sue if any resulting offspring turn out to have genetic diseases, and that the bank cannot promise that I would get pregnant. I had heard of women who buy twelve or fifteen vials of their chosen donor's sperm, hoarding as much of it as they can get. But at $195 each—which was apparently the going rate for sperm—I decided to buy two and hope for the best.

I picked up the phone, Visa card in hand.

"He's gone," the woman at the sperm bank said. Gone? My guy was out of stock. I felt as if I'd been stood up. I went back to the catalogue to pick another.

It's a bizarre roll of the dice, this business of shopping for sperm. I was picking genes based on a paragraph of personal description and a short family medical history. I realized it was unlikely, and perhaps undesirable, that I would ever meet the donor. I acknowledged that he might be unhappy if he knew that his sperm went to a lesbian. But, on some level, I still wanted to have a sense of who this person was. I tried to read between the lines, gleaning bits of personality from the short notes, looking for character in an inference. While it's true that the sperm was just the genetic key required to unlock my egg, it is also true that within this anonymous donor's intertwined ribbons of DNA were generations of love and hate and history that neither Jane, nor I, nor our child would likely ever know.

Finally, I found another donor who seemed to fit the bill. He came from the same mishmash of European heritage as Jane, had completed a master's degree, and had parents who were both university professors. He was a practicing Christian, which could mean anything, so I chose to assume that he was not a fundamentalist. I ordered two vials and paid the additional $50 to have the sperm delivered in casks of liquid nitrogen to my doctor's office. Then, I sat back and waited for my egg.

Jane and I had decided to have the insemination done at a clinic that specialized in obstetrics and infertility, even though I felt like an interloper there. I had no reason to think that I was infertile, other than the obvious reality that Jane and I just couldn't seem to get pregnant on our own. My regular physician, a family practice doctor, didn't do inseminations. Only one doctor at the clinic did them at all and, it turned out, only during standard clinic hours. Ovulate on a Sunday or a holiday and you were out of luck.

At our first appointment at the fertility clinic, the doctor came into the exam room where Jane and I waited for him. He was a big man with broad shoulders and brown, curly hair who wanted to get right down to the business of our hour-long intake interview and exam.

He began by asking me a series of questions: age, profession, menstrual history. He carefully wrote the answers to each question on a yellow legal pad. "We'll have you do some tests before we get started to make sure everything's in order," he said. "That will save time later." He handed me a sheet of information entitled Patient Infertility Evaluation. He had helpfully marked big X's through the sections on semen analysis and postcoital analysis, lest I be confused. "We'll make sure your FSH, estradiol, prolactin, and progesterone are all OK," he said. Glancing at the information sheet in my hand, I saw that FSH is my follicle-stimulating hormone, one of the raft of proteins and chemicals that all need to come together to make pregnancy work.

The various tests that he recommended had to be conducted on specific days of my menstrual cycle. The doctor rattled off instructions. "Call the clinic on day one of your next cycle. We'll do a blood test on day three. We need to check the progesterone eight days after your next LH surge." The LH surge, I knew from my reading, is the body's release of luteinizing hormone that occurs about a day before ovulation. He also wanted me to do two ultrasounds a few days apart to make sure that my eggs were developing and releasing on schedule.

"Go to the drugstore and get yourself a Clear Plan Easy kit," he went on. Clear Plan Easy is an over-the-counter package of urine tests that would tell me if my LH had, in fact, surged. "You can get a generic brand," he added, "but it won't be as good. Then start testing your urine on day eight of your cycle. Don't use the first urine of the day. Use the second, but be sure it's before noon."

Good Lord. And to think other people just have sex.

"Having a baby is a big responsibility," the doctor said as he capped his pen, tapped it twice on his pad, and returned it to his shirt pocket. I could almost hear Jane's eyes roll.

Three weeks after ordering sperm, I was back at the clinic. My tests all indicated that I was normal. I had confirmed with the help of Clear Plan Easy that my egg was about to roll down one of my fallopian tubes. The sperm I had selected passed muster with the nurse, who checked a couple of droplets under the microscope to make sure that it emerged from its deep freeze without compromising its motility. Everything was ready.

I lay in the bright exam room waiting to be impregnated with the sperm of a complete stranger by a perky nurse whom I had just met. The procedure went something like this: Lie on the table with my feet in the stirrups while the nurse inserts a catheter into the cervix. Lie there some more while she tries another catheter because the first one couldn't find the opening to the uterus. Lie there some more while she tries a second speculum in case the first one was blocking the entrance. Lie there some more and think about how it feels remarkably like I have a pair of garden trowels stuck inside me. Lie there some more while she tries catheter number three. Keep lying there while she goes to get backup. Shirley, a much older and more experienced nurse, came into the room.

"We're having some trouble, are we?" Shirley asked. She took over and within a few seconds announced mission accomplished. "Are you hoping for a boy or a girl?" she asked. I opened my mouth to answer, but nothing came out. My God, a baby.

Jane sat on a chair next to the exam table where I lay. I was so grateful that we were doing this at a time and place where I didn't have to pretend to be straight and single—or worse, straight and married. Until relatively recently, fertility clinics have been the domain of heterosexual women and their slightly embarrassed husbands. But there we were in our very mainstream, suburban clinic in Edina, Minnesota, with its flouncy valences on the windows and its medical art on the walls—large geometrical shapes in lots of pinks and light blues—and the nurses seemed to think it was just great that a couple of lesbians wanted to get pregnant.

Lying on my back on the exam table, I thought about these little pioneers in my uterus, venturing where no sperm had gone before. I felt weirdly relaxed. I had been afraid that I would come to this point and panic, suddenly realizing that I was hurtling down a highway with no remaining exits. But in that moment, I felt like it was a fine thing that we were doing. I leaned over the edge of the table and kissed my Jane. I held her hand, stroked her hair. We were part of intersecting modern phenomena: medically assisted conception and the so-called gayby boom. But we were also part of a timeless tradition: two people coming together in love, hoping to make a new life. The possibility of becoming pregnant felt like venturing into a rushing stream, not knowing where the current would take us. I closed my eyes and trusted that there were stepping stones under the water, made of history and dreams, and that our feet would find them.

[IV]

Eight weeks later, I was back on the exam table, having come up unpregnant after the first two rounds. On the advice of my doctor, who promised a "bigger bang for the buck," I was inseminating two times per ovulatory cycle, making this my fifth go at it. I had decided to try a new donor in the hope that I might have better luck. This one was a medical student, which led me to believe that his sperm might have some special insider knowledge about how to penetrate an egg. He enjoyed cross-country running and skiing, and he was right-handed. He wanted to be married and have a family. So did I.

I felt a pinch as the catheter negotiated its way through my cervix.

"Try a little visualization," the nurse said. I closed my eyes and imagined my egg opening for the sperm. And then I began to worry. I worried that my egg was a separatist lesbian egg that would herd all the little swimmers back to the cervical opening and spit them out while delivering a little lecture on patriarchal hegemony. I opened my eyes.

As always, the nurse left the room after finishing her part of the operation, waving her crossed fingers in the air and wishing me luck. I lay on my back, watching the clock, waiting for ten minutes to tick by until I could get up, put on my pants, and go to work.

Truthfully, even on the fifth go-round, I was still a little surprised to be in that room, on the exam table, chock full of sperm. Although Jane and I had talked about having a child for ten years, there is a vast chasm between talking and trying. Somewhere along the line, despite all of our digressions and stalls, our talk turned from hypothesis to plan, from idea to action.

The fact that we talked about it for ten years surprised me in and of itself because it could have been so much longer. Jane and I can talk and talk and talk. We fell in love talking. We came to know each other by talking. We entertain and annoy each other by talking. Talking is how we explain ourselves to ourselves. It is how we have imagined and created our relationship from the first day we met.

"*Heute abend habe ich Jane Miller kennengelernt*," I wrote in my journal just a few hours after meeting Jane for the first time. "Tonight I met Jane Miller." We were both nineteen. I was just a few weeks back from a year in Germany. She was a sophomore and I was a freshman at DePauw University in the heart of Indiana's corn and pig country. A professor whom we both knew, who had romantic, quasi-Hellenic notions about mentorship, suggested that we might like each other. Jane left a yellow Post-It on my door, with a note inviting me to stop by her dorm room. I still have the Post-It, perforated with thumbtack holes and tucked away in a box on my bookcase.

Within a few minutes of meeting, I discovered that Jane spoke German. I was full of German words, German ideas, German food, and German resentments about America. My dorm, with its four floors of freshman girls nearly entirely obsessed with which sorority they would join, was a throwback to Eisenhower's America. When I met Jane, I was transported back to the pastures and windmills and pubs of Emsland.

That first night, we talked for hours. We talked about Germany and where we had traveled and where we might like to go some day. We talked about sororities and fraternities, about President Reagan and nuclear weapons and whether might, in fact, makes right. Every day after that, we talked. About Chinua Achebe and Marge Piercy and Rita Mae Brown and Saul Alinsky. About Jane's major, anthropology. About Margaret Mead and how she had attended DePauw for one utterly miserable year. About movies. About our political science class and the myth and ideology of American public life. About how we'd like to go to New Zealand to shear sheep, despite the fact that our familiarity with sheep began and ended at wearing sweaters. We went for walks, lay in the lounge, sat at the sandwich shop, lingered in the cafeteria. We lay on Jane's bed listening to endless repetitions of Don McLean's *American Pie*. We spent so much time enrapt in each other that suspicions sprouted like weeds. Long before it ever happened, there were rumors that we had been seen kissing in the stairwell or the theater or the commons. But we weren't kissing; we were talking, although in our case, one was just a prelude to the other.

Over the course of two years, we talked ourselves into a new vision of our future. We began to imagine a future that contained both of us, together, indefinitely. The river of conversation had no visible end. We began to believe that we could talk for the rest of our lives. Maybe that was our first step toward babymaking.

[V]

Trying to conceive is the perfect pastime for the obsessive. It's a full-time hobby: testing temperatures, examining mucus, talking with other trying-to-conceive (that's "ttc" to those in the know) women online, reading books, waiting, getting the sperm inside, waiting some more. I spent extraordinary amounts of time trying to discern the mercurial moods of my reproductive organs. Because I start almost every project with a book, I bought *Taking Charge of Your Fertility* a few months before I started inseminating. On its advice, I began to chart my basal, or waking, temperature. Supposedly, I would be able to discern a regular pattern that would help me figure out when I was about to ovulate. My waking temperature should hover around ninety-seven degrees prior to ovulation and then should bounce up to something closer to ninety-eight after the egg emerged. The book assured me that charting my basal temperature would be not only easy, but also fun.

Every morning, when I first awoke, I reached gingerly for the thermometer, trying not to raise my shoulders, as the book warned me that any unnecessary movement could skew the result. I slipped the thermometer into my mouth and lay still, thinking quietly about ovulation. Apparently, other women enjoy this. Apparently, other women's temperatures have patterns. Mine, carefully charted on graph paper, looked more like an EKG gone bad. There were many possible reasons for this. Maybe I had been hot that night, or restless, or had a bad dream, or recklessly breaking all the rules, had gotten up to pee. Or maybe, I feared, I have no pattern. Maybe the rhythm of my ovaries was as haphazard as the rhythm of my dancing.

Reading on in *Taking Charge*, I discovered that I could follow my cycle better if I also monitored my cervical mucus. The book urged me to pay attention to the ways in which my mucus changed throughout the month, to watch for the clear, stretchy, slippery "egg white" that signals fertility. I learned that mucus is not, in fact, mucusy and gross—it's beautiful, the very stuff of life. A magnified photo of cervical mucus demonstrated the "beautiful ferning pattern" that appears during ovulation. This is stuff that I had thoughtlessly been wiping off my panties for years. Now, I discovered that it really is kind of pretty, at least under a microscope.

I became a regular in the feminine hygiene aisle at Walgreen's, buying my Clear Plan Easy ovulation predictor kits, with their seven plastic sticks promising to tell me when I was most likely to conceive. I went through this enough times to know that I seemed to ovulate around day thirteen of my cycle, but I didn't want to miss an early escapee, so I took a Clear Plan Easy stick to work with me each day beginning on day ten. Midmorning, I snagged a Styrofoam cup from the kitchen and tried to walk discreetly to the bathroom, cup in hand. Once there, I collected some urine, dipped the stick, and sat in the stall, waiting five minutes for the result. I tracked the results in my date book, along with little notations about the state of my mucus: "D" meant dry; "little EW" meant there was a little bit of the desired egg white mucus. Then there were the "tons EW" days.

The more I did this, the more I came to believe that my body follows rhythms and rules of its own devising. Some months, I got a strong and clear read of impending ovulation. Other months, I got two days of positives, as though my egg was peeking her head out of the fallopian tube but then scooting back inside to gather courage before braving the trip. Perhaps I was inseminating too early. Or maybe I was doing it too late. I tried to jimmy the schedule, planning inseminations a little earlier or a little later than recommended, in the hope of snaring an egg.

The nurse at my clinic began to talk with me about Clomid. She explained that it is a hyperovulatory drug. It would make me produce more eggs (and, possibly, more babies). But, I thought, we don't know that ovulation, or the lack of it, is my problem. If we don't know what the problem is, then we don't know that throwing Clomid at it will help. It seemed to me like putting something bigger in the path of pregnancy. But if pregnancy got off at an earlier exit, my inflated roadblock would do no good. Plus, I had a horror of the Multiple Birth. I had a nightmarish vision of becoming a human-interest story on the ten o'clock news: Lesbian Mom Has Litter. The camera would pan across seven kids, lined up in high chairs, waiting for the dazed and confused mother to wipe their drooling mouths.

I told the nurse I would think about it.

[VI]

After a few more months of—not to be harsh—FAILURE, Jane and I persuaded ourselves that we might have better luck if we tried inseminating at home. We had talked to other women who had done this, some successfully and some not. We also browsed the

Internet, looking for the occasional lesbians amidst the scores of women whose virtual conversations about conception oozed hope and desperation.

There is an entire subgenre of lesbian lore about home insemination. It begins with those who used the turkey-baster method—classically, a little sperm in a shot glass from an obliging gay friend, and use of the baster to get it inside the mother wannabe. Some women supplement this method with techniques of their own devising. We know one woman who stood on her head in her bedroom after her partner inseminated her with their baster, on the assumption that turning upside down could only help. The turkey-baster method is primitive, but it does work, even if it consigns you to a lifetime of eating dry turkey.

We know another couple who created a whole ceremony around their at-home insemination. They set up a kind of altar in their bedroom and arranged upon it pictures and symbols of people and places that were meaningful to them, that represented family and home. They laid out a sheaf of wheat to represent fertility. They thought fertile thoughts. Apparently it worked: they have two kids.

I read on one of the online fertility discussions that some of the problems we are having could be linked to the inherent stress of inseminating in a doctor's office. I didn't feel especially stressed when I was at the clinic, or at least I didn't think I did, but maybe my eggs felt pressured. Perhaps the comfort of our own bed, the mewling of our own cats, and the privacy of our own room would help my egg feel more secure. And, even though there would be a vat of liquid nitrogen sitting in the middle of the room, Jane and I wanted to try to capture some of the intimacy that is supposed to go with getting pregnant. We wanted to make love.

Our regular clinic did not allow us to get a jug of sperm to go, although the sperm bank was happy to ship to any doctor. We arranged for the shipment to go to another clinic, under the authorization of a gynecologist who was a friend of ours. When it arrived,

Jane and I went together to pick up the delivery. There is a certain self-consciousness that inherently accompanies carrying around a vat of sperm. The vat itself was large, about the size of a desktop computer, and surprisingly heavy, considering that the only thing of value that it contained was a two-inch plastic vial of sperm. Jane and I were not used to driving frozen sperm around town, so we drove home directly and carefully, lest we hit a bump and create an embarrassing hazmat spill.

Jane lugged the jug of sperm into our house and up the stairs to our bedroom. She put it on the floor in the middle of the room. We were excited and a little giddy, like schoolgirls who just got hold of *The Joy of Sex*.

"How do you want to do this?" I asked.

"Well, I don't know," Jane said. "Why don't we try to relax?" She sat on the edge of the bed next to me. She gave me a kiss. I put my arms around her. We scooched into the center of the bed and lay down. She kissed my lips, my eyes. I ran my hands through her hair. She reached her hands under my shirt, stroking my waist and nuzzling my neck. I unbuttoned her blouse. My hands slid toward the top of her jeans.

Meanwhile, the vat of liquid nitrogen stood sentinel in the middle of the room. It was like a third person—both anonymous donor and potential child—standing on the rug, staring at us.

I rolled Jane over so that I faced the other direction. All I could think about was sperm. This is not what a lesbian generally wants in bed.

I sat up. "Maybe we should just do the deed," I said. Jane got up and pulled out the set of instructions and disposable catheter that came with the sperm. We had purchased a box of latex gloves that waited on top of the dresser.

"OK," Jane said. "Let's get down to business."

She pulled on a pair of gloves. I took off my pants and sat on the bed, watching Jane and trying to feel relaxed and fertile.

Jane removed the catheter from its plastic packaging. She spread the Handling/Thawing Instructions for Cryopreserved Semen on the floor next to the nitrogen. She unscrewed the top of the canister, lifted it off, and pulled out the metal cane holding our vial of sperm. She checked the number on the side, ensuring that, in fact, we had sperm from the right guy. Holding the vial of sperm in the air with her right hand, she picked up the instructions in her left and began to read.

"Do not lift the top of the canes above the top of the liquid nitrogen container opening, this may result in premature thawing."

"Oops," she said.

I imagined the sperm wilting away like the sea monkeys that I kept in recycled peanut butter jars when I was a child. They were going belly up.

In an effort at damage control, she wrapped the vial in a cloth towel for twenty seconds as the instructions advised, and then unwrapped it and set it on the dresser to thaw.

"Safety glasses are highly recommended," she read. Oops, again.

After the thawing period was presumably complete, Jane drew the sperm into a catheter and came over to the bed. I lay back on the pillows, spread my legs, and awaited delivery.

"God, this is weird," Jane said. She inserted the catheter and released the sperm, while I hoped that enough sea monkeys were still alive and sufficiently energized to make the trip north.

When she was done, Jane set the catheter and empty vial on the dresser and climbed into bed next to me. I put my arm around her and we lay still against the pillows. I watched the afternoon sky through the window as it grew dark.

Insemination is not romantic. Latex gloves and instruction sheets put a distinct damper on intimacy. It is a procreative mixed metaphor, a sentence that doesn't add up.

But there was still a sweetness, a tender softness in lying together. Jane nestled her head against my shoulder.

"I love you," she whispered.

"I love you, too."

[VII]

We told very few people about our attempts to get pregnant. My sister knew and periodically asked for updates on the "B Project," as she called it. A smattering of friends knew, but that was it. Telling raises expectations, both in us and of us. We had no baby to announce, just lots of endlessly fascinating detail about mucus.

We did tell our friends, Andrew and Mark, because they were our dearest friends. For the past several years, we had eaten dinner with them once a week, passing terrines of polenta, plates of roast chicken, slabs of lasagna. The dinners were like family dinners, but more fun. Andrew and Mark were among the first people we met when we moved to Minnesota from New York in the early nineties. At the time, we attended the same church. We went to movies, played cards, went canoeing and skiing, and traveled together. When we got together, we talked about this and that: work, family, food, wine, books. Sometimes we got on each others' nerves, but every week we came back for more. We laughed. We fit each other.

Between dinners, Jane and I imagined what it would be like when we had a baby. We knew other couples who had arranged shared child care, almost to the extent of co-parenting, with their closest friends. We assumed that the weekly dinners would continue, with the addition of a high chair.

Both Andrew and Mark were devoted to family, in some ways far more than either Jane or I. They loved to tell stories about learning to play poker with Grandma, going to the beach house with all the aunts and cousins, or making homemade Christmas gifts for their siblings. Andrew rearranged his work schedule one summer so that he could take a day off every week to care for the young daughter of good friends. Each winter, they cooked a tub of chili and hosted a neighborhood block party, making a special point of walking with the elderly folks to ensure they didn't slip on the ice.

"God, they're so *good*," Jane said one night as we walked home from their house, our stomachs full of bratwurst and potato salad.

Our great hope was that we would have a child and they would adopt one, that our kids would grow up together, that we would vacation together, and that we would all bake cookies together, Andrew and Mark virtuously taking plates of goodies around to the neighbors while Jane and I stood in the kitchen with our kid, licking the crumbs off our chins.

[VIII]

Finally, one day, I thought I might really be pregnant. This worried me because I could be wrong. And it worried me because I could be right, which would be both terrifying and exciting, which would turn my entire world upside down, grip it by the ankles, and shake it. Throughout all the inseminations, I had wondered what I really want. Did I really want to have a child? Did I really want not to have a child? Was this an acceptable question to ask while trying to get pregnant? To be honest, I still didn't know for sure.

I knew that you're not pregnant just because you "feel" that way, but I began having symptoms that indicated that I might, conceivably, have conceived. Jane told me I was more moody than usual, which would be a lot. I was exhausted. I also had light cramps, starting about two days after insemination and continuing as a sort of persistent whisper. They were quiet and mild, but they lasted for several days, appearing and disappearing and then reappearing. Perhaps it was gas, I thought. Perhaps it was early menstrual cramping. Perhaps it was imaginary. Or perhaps it was the Speck looking for a good spot to burrow.

But I was wrong. Premenstrual mania set in: chocolate craving, cramping, late afternoon depression, and the emergence of my Inner Bitch. I made a desperate run to the store to get not one but two packages of my favorite chocolate cookies—Le Petite Ecolier—the Little Schoolboy. I sat in the car, crying and tearing the cellophane off the plastic tray that cradled the Schoolboys. Saltwater tears ran down my cheeks. I spilled the cookies into my lap. And I bit their smiling heads off.

That night, I sat on the sofa and watched the crescent moon, the kind that children like to draw. The night sky was the color of Crayola's midnight blue: not yet black, a little past navy. I had spent a year and a half trying to get pregnant, but not getting pregnant. I had monitored the cycles through which my body moved, measured temperatures, tested hormone levels, and paid undue attention to mucus. I had charted and graphed and recorded notes, and all that came of it was a stack of charts and graphs and notes.

My reflection hovered in the window in front of the moon. My hair was messy, as usual. I looked at my face and the scar on my forehead where I landed repeatedly as a sadly clumsy four-year-old. I looked at the lopsided curve of my waist and the little plums of breasts. I was not pregnant, but, it turned out, I wanted to be.

TWO

No Waiting, Womb Two

[1]

I WAKE UP IN THE MIDDLE of the night and look at the clock. Two-thirty. I could be getting up now for a nighttime feeding. I could be listening to the electronic baby monitor, obsessively tuned to my child's breathing. I could be a mom.

How in the world do I begin to internalize the fact that Jane is truly, actually, genuinely pregnant? How do I begin to understand that it is real, that it is happening to me and to us? It is harder to wrap your mind around pregnancy when you are not pregnant yourself, a fact that makes me feel a sudden empathy for men. Jane is wrapping her body around our future baby, and her mind follows. She is beginning to notice and comment on early physical changes. Her breasts are blossoming. She is constantly exhausted. She craves grilled meat and eats it like a Viking. I experience all of this only vicariously. I see the changes, but I don't feel them.

The numbers on the clock keep turning over. 2:46. We have about 38 weeks to go. That's 266 more days. And 266 more nights. That's a mere 6,384 hours. 383,040 minutes.

Make that 383,039.

We had talked about the possibility of becoming parents for so long. I thought that by the time I reached this point, if in fact I ever did, I would surely be ready. Instead, I feel like I have jumped off a cliff. I am in free fall. I am flying.

2:52. I imagine the three of us decorating a Christmas tree.

Christmas music plays on the stereo. Our little girl or little boy will be excited about Santa Claus and snow and reindeer. We'll hang the ornaments on the tree, including the stuffed red elf that I got from my best friend in kindergarten. I'll help our child put out a plate of cookies for Santa, and later I'll leave a nice thank-you note amidst the crumbs, just like Santa did at our house every year.

2:56. My God, I haven't changed a diaper in twenty years.

3:02. What the fuck are we doing???

3:03. Whose idea was this, anyway?

Jane's breath rides up and down, deep into herself, then long and slow out of herself. Inside her body, the factory is in its third shift, cells diligently dividing into a new brain, a new heart, a child. I hold my breath and listen for the sounds of change.

3:11. I imagine myself sitting in a rocking chair, in the middle of the night, holding our baby. Stroking our baby's head. Kissing our baby's foot.

I close my eyes and wait for sleep.

[11]

It was Thanksgiving that got us into this. We had driven to the southern border of Indiana, way down yonder on the banks of the Ohio River, to spend the holiday with Jane's family. Everyone gathered at her parents' house: Jane's two sisters and brother, all at least fourteen years her senior, their spouses, most of their children, and now, their grandchildren. Jane's parents have segued comfortably from parenthood to grandparenthood to great-grandparenthood, doing basically what they always did before, but progressively less of it. Her mother pretended to direct activity in the kitchen. Her father said grace and poured wine from a box. Other than the time dedicated to laying out the turkey, eating the turkey, and cleaning up after the turkey, most of the holiday was spent drinking budget wine, watching television, and passing around the newest great-grandbaby, who spent most of her holiday wailing.

On the way back, somewhere in central Illinois, Jane crumpled the wrapper from her Subway Veggie Delite, emptied the last shards of potato chips from their bag, licked her fingers, and then wiped them on a paper napkin. She brushed the remaining crumbs from her lap. She lifted the glass of Sprite from the cup holder and took a sip.

Outside, the sky was as flat and gray as the highway. The trees were mostly bare, a few clinging with tired fingers to clusters of dry leaves. The fields lay cold and still. We had been driving for about six hours and had another seven to go.

"I'm willing to try," Jane said.

"Uh-huh," I said. "Try what?" I glanced at her. She sat in the passenger seat, dressed in jeans, a purple turtleneck, and a cardigan sweater. Her brown hair was clipped into a barrette. Her eyes, dark like chocolate, looked at me.

"Getting pregnant," Jane answered.

When we go on car trips, I love to talk about Big Issues. I don't really care what the topic is, as long as it's both meaty and personal. Like, where we want to be in five years. Or trips we want to take. Or family concerns. Or how to find a better balance between work and the rest of living. Jane dislikes Big Issues as much as I love them. When we start on a trip, after we have made our obligatory stops for coffee and tea and baked goods, I will announce that it is time for Big Issues. "Oh, God," Jane groans. "Can't we just talk? Or listen to music?" Or, she adds hopefully, "you could drive and I could sleep?" The last thing I expected from her was what she had just given me: the Mother of All Big Issues. I barely knew what to say.

"Really?"

She nodded.

I knew that Jane wanted to have a child, but I also knew that she had not been interested in getting pregnant herself until, well, apparently just that moment. She shied away from the realities of pregnancy: sciatica, nausea, breasts that feel like overpumped tires, birth. She regularly insisted that evolution must have goofed, that, in her words, the mammalian method of getting the baby out can't possibly be right. She struggled to imagine herself attached to a fetus, either physically or emotionally. She was unwilling to hand her body over to unknown forces for nine months.

"Are you serious?" I asked her.

She nodded again, smiling. She had made up her mind. I was stunned.

After I repeatedly tried and failed to get pregnant, we considered our options, although admittedly not with much diligence. We briefly considered the suggestion by the nurse at my fertility clinic to try hormone shots with the goal of kicking my reproductive system into overdrive. We both worried about the long-term impact, especially considering the cancer that ran in my family. It wasn't something I wanted to do, and Jane flatly refused to give me the injections which, given the necessary timing, had to be done at home. "We'll teach you how to do it," the nurse told us, adding, helpfully, that Jane could practice on an orange.

Over the next several months, we made a quarter-hearted exploration of adoption. We attended introductory sessions at two agencies, feeling like infiltrators in the rooms full of eager couples seated Husband, Wife, Husband, Wife. We quickly found things not to like. One agency told us that they do occasionally place children in homes with gay couples but would prefer that it not be too public because the board of directors remains "unresolved" about gay parenthood. A social worker at a different agency told us that they are absolutely happy to include gay couples in the book of potential adoptive parents that birth mothers review prior to entering into an open adoption. "In fact, we have some gay couples now," she said. "They just haven't been selected yet."

I made a few forays onto the Internet that were mostly disheartening. I discovered a site where I could "Browse the Children," all 126 pages of them. I discovered that if I typed in "adoption + Minnesota," I got sites for adoption agencies and the local Humane Society. I visited the site for Minnesota's Waiting Children and read the biographical paragraphs written by social workers trying to be upbeat while still adhering roughly to truth-in-advertising guidelines. "Bobby loves pizza and football. He struggles with prolonged anger outbursts." "Anna has pretty red hair. She needs a great deal of redirection by experienced and very patient parents." We were completely out of our league.

We talked about trying to do an international adoption. We knew people who had adopted from Guatemala or China or Colombia, but we were also aware that, among those countries willing to accept unmarried parents, several had become more restrictive as a means of shutting out gay couples. And then there was the expense, easily running to $15,000 or more.

Meanwhile, Jane began to volunteer at a local crisis nursery, spending a couple of hours every week playing with or feeding or holding the kids while they waited for their parents to emerge from whatever meltdown they were negotiating that day. Some of the children were new each time; others were regulars, but all were lucky, relatively speaking. They had parents with the wherewithal to get their kids to a place that would care for them. Jane came back from her visits talking about Basil, who loved to play kitty, or Jasmine, who just wanted to be rocked, or DeShawn, who couldn't abide the taste of the donated fish sticks the crisis nursery served for dinner.

We stalled, but without really looking, we were inching closer. We repeatedly reviewed and discarded the various options. Maybe we knew all along that Jane would do it in the end.

"I'm serious," Jane said finally, as I continued driving north.

"I've realized that I want a baby and I want one who is biologically related. I guess I just would have preferred to have it delivered to the door."

"I'd do it if I could," I said.

"I know."

"When do you want to start trying?"

"I'm ready."

This is classic Jane. I will yatter obsessively for months as I wade through a decision, making her sit through every agonizing twist and turn. Jane gestates silently until her decision pops out whole.

I wanted to dissect this deliciously big Big Issue. My mind was racing. I had Jane trapped in the car for the next seven hours, maybe eight if I drove just under the speed limit. I thought back to the early days of my inseminations, recreating the order of events. We needed to call the doctor's office. We needed to get on the Internet and review the sperm catalogue. We needed to register Jane at the sperm bank. We needed to figure out when she ovulates. I was just warming up, about to launch in. As I opened my mouth to begin, Jane reached over to the dashboard.

"Let's see what's on the radio," she said.

[IIII]

Jane is making a baby and I am making lists. I am basically clueless about pregnancy, until now having really only paid attention to conception. I had no idea how much there is to do, and only nine months—eight and a half, actually—to do it in. We have to decide on an ob-gyn. We have to choose a hospital. We have to find out when we're supposed to take childbirth classes. We have to choose a crib. We have to figure out what we need for the first few weeks of Baby's life. We have to find a lawyer so that I can get a second-parent adoption set in motion. We (well, I) have to learn how to put on a diaper. We have to choose between cloth and disposable. We have to go to the bookstore. We have to nap. We have to tell our parents.

And telling our parents is an issue unto itself. It's a reality that not all parents are excited to hear that their lesbian daughter is pregnant. We know a depressing number of people whose parents have been upset by the news, feeling that their future grandchild will be too vulnerable, too stigmatized, too *influenced*. In most cases, but certainly not all, Grandma and Grandpa get over their reservations when the baby arrives. Suddenly, the actual infant is more important than numinous fears that she will be dressed by her mommies in little lavender onesies that say in sparkly letters, "How dare you presume I'm heterosexual!" When one friend told her parents that she and her partner were thinking about having a child, her father gave her a pained look and asked, "Do you know of anyone else who has ever done *anything* like that?"

Actually, yes.

According to people who spend time researching these things, there is a "gayby boom" going on. Estimates of the number of kids being raised by gay, lesbian, bisexual, or transgender parents range widely. On the low end, the U.S. Census, which arrives at its number by tracking self-reporting "unmarried partner" households, estimated in 2000 that these households included about 270,000 children nationwide. But census counts of the gay community are notoriously low and also overlook families with bisexual, transgender, or even single gay or lesbian parents. On the high end, the American Academy of Pediatrics estimates that between one million and nine million children under the age of eighteen live with gay or lesbian parents. Certainly, many of these kids were born through heterosexual relationships, and others were adopted. But an increasing number are the result of some form of assisted reproduction. People in the gay community—especially lesbians, but increasingly also gay men—are assuming that they can have children. This is a sea change. Just twenty or so years earlier, coming out generally meant letting go of expectations of parenthood. There have always been gay men and lesbians who didn't want children, of course, just as there have always been straight men and women (some of them parents) who don't. But there have always been others who have wanted it, sometimes deeply and desperately. A gay male friend, about ten years older than I, told me once that he became very depressed when he realized that he was gay because he was certain that it meant he would never become a father. And, in fact, he never has.

Historically, the gay community as a whole has compensated for its lack of procreation by more or less ignoring children. Our most distinctive institutions have traditionally been bars. We have been defined by our sexuality and have often played to type, building a culture—with all its camp and art, its politics and pathos—that emphasizes sex. We spend our money on travel and cars and home renovations. We devote ourselves to our jobs, to our gardens, to volunteer work, to our pets. Only recently has the focus begun to shift to marriage and, for a subset of the community, to kids.

Still, there are and always have been plenty of individual gay men and lesbians who have forged generous and affirming relationships with children. For generations, there have been the maiden aunts and bachelor uncles who serve as confidantes, alternative role models, or even surrogate parents. Jane and I know several couples who have become informal foster parents or extremely engaged godparents, or who have taken in stray kids who needed some supportive adults in their lives. Until relatively recently, however, our families have existed on the margins of kinship and many of our children have been the children of other people.

Jane and I are not concerned that our families will disapprove of her pregnancy, but we are still not certain how they will react. I learned by coming out, when I blithely expected my parents to cheer the news, that it's best not to make assumptions. Our parents are fine with our relationship now, having long ago worked out any initial concerns they might have had about us suddenly deciding to hang around in seedy bars and join all-women biker gangs. Some members of my family know that I tried to get pregnant, but it is not something we have discussed in any open way with Jane's family. We don't have to deal with the pressure of producing a grandchild on someone else's schedule, but we also aren't sure if it has really even registered with her family that we might have a kid one day.

A week after Jane takes the pregnancy test, she decides to call her parents. We know that the conventional wisdom is to wait three months, to get around the miscarriage window. But this is information that can no longer be contained. Her mother, Mary, picks up the phone and Jane tells her the news.

"You've known for a *week* and you didn't call me?" Mary responds. So much for the three-month window. I listen to Jane's responses as her mother begins the Litany of Maternal Questions.

"I'm due in mid-March," Jane says.

"I'm looking for a doctor. I've got a good recommendation from a friend."

"No, I'm not really sick. Just exhausted."

"Oh, yeah, I'm sleeping. All the time, in fact."

A few minutes into the conversation, I realize that Mary is planning her pilgrimage to the birth site. "Of course you can come in March, Mama," Jane says. "You can be there in the delivery room." I gasp. Jane looks at my face and convulses into a fit of silent giggles. She is loving every minute of this, setting delicious bait for everyone around her and waiting to see who will grab it first.

I imagine Mary in the delivery room. Now in her mid-seventies, her favorite activity is to make friends. She grew up in small-town South Dakota and is a fusion of the upper midwesterner's aversion to strong emotion and the small-town resident's love of visiting. Take her anywhere and she begins to chat with people as though they were simply picking up a long-forgotten conversation. Take her anywhere, in fact, and she has a tendency to wander off in whatever direction looks like it might have the most interesting people. I have a disturbing image of finding her in someone else's birthing room, sitting at the laboring woman's bedside, chatting: "You're doing great, honey. My daughter's just down the hall. You two should meet. But not right now, of course."

After she has exhausted her list of questions, Mary hands the phone to Jane's father, Larry. In all the years that I have been with Jane, I have never seen her mother cry, but I have seen her father cry often. With age, he has become soft, despite his heritage. An Iowa German, Larry is as much a product of the gridded midwestern town as Mary is a child of the open Dakota plain. After he sold the moving business that he ran for years, he became a licensed minister, taking interim churches across rural southern Indiana for the United Church of Christ. Larry believes in ambition and structure and hard work and duty. Mary believes in microwave meals and chatting and the Cubs. Sniffling into the phone, Jane's father tells her that the family has discussed for years whether or not we would have a baby.

"You've *what?*" Jane spits out. This comes as a complete shock. We thought that her pregnancy would surprise them. Now we find out that they've been expecting this, just biding their time.

Next, I dial the phone. My father, who lives in Ohio, answers after three rings. He knows that I had tried to get pregnant and that it didn't take. I had stopped trying by the time I told him, but he responded anyway by offering to "check for resources" in Ohio, whatever that means, presumably to find out if someone there knew something more about assisted reproduction than they know in Minnesota. It made perfect sense to him, fitting neatly into his world view, absorbed in 1940s Iowa, in which everyone knows each other, and they all sit around the bandstand on Saturday nights eating peppermint ice cream. If his daughter needs help, by golly, he'll ask around until he finds it.

The entire time I lived at home, my father was a United Methodist minister, leaving the pastorate on the cusp of retirement, at just about the same time that Jane's father entered it. Church runs thick in my family. When my parents divorced after a quarter-century of marriage, my mother went to seminary herself. My uncle is a minister, as are some once- or twice-removed cousins and some members of the family who never left Germany for the New World. Those who aren't clergy are active churchgoers, Altar Guilders, seminary professors, and choir members. I went to seminary myself, in part because it seemed like the natural progression of things.

For years, I could barely separate the concepts of father and minister, so fused were they after two decades of watching him every Sunday morning as he raised his robed arms and invited us to stand as we are able. But now, freed from the politics and the expectations and the liturgies of the church, he is increasingly just my dad—the guy who effuses about his favorite grocery store because he can get everything from zucchini to jeans really cheap, who loves his gym because "you can use as many towels as you want," and who checks for insemination resources for his daughter.

"I have some news," I say. "Jane's pregnant." There is momentary stunned silence.

"Jane?" he asks, processing the information.

"Yup, Jane," I repeat. My partner. My de facto wife.

He begins to ask questions, rapid fire.

How's she doing? Fine.

Do you want to know the gender of the baby? Yes.

How old are you two? Thirty-seven.

What will your status be? I'll do a second-parent adoption, I say. Lots of those are granted in our county every year, I add. I'm punting when I say this. I really don't know how many gay and lesbian adoptions are granted and whether any are denied. But this hardly seems time to split hairs.

Another pause. Finally he asks, "How did you do it?" Well, Dad, I think, we bought sperm over the Internet. It sounds like we went to eBay.

"We went to the same fertility clinic where I went," I say. "We bought sperm from an anonymous donor at a sperm bank."

I suggest to him that he brush up on his grandfatherly skills. Jane's parents are old hands at grandparenting and even at great-grandparenting. This baby will have a special status in her family largely because of its procrastination; barring huge surprises and a few medical miracles, it will be the last grandchild. My parents, on the other hand, have not been down this road before.

"I'm going to be a grandfather," he says. I can hear his grin. The wheels are turning. He is beginning to plan fishing trips and card games with this baby who doesn't even have fingers yet. He is calculating how often he and my stepmother, Nan, can come to visit. He is thinking about when the house next door might go up for sale.

"You need to understand that you may think you know me and you may think you know Nan," he says, "but when you make us grandparents, we become something altogether different. It's a whole new ballgame."

[IV]

"How are you preparing?" asks Rebecca, our friend and sometime minister, on the weeks when we actually make it to church. The three of us are sitting around our dining-room table, eating pizza. No one has yet asked us quite this question. The few friends whom we have told about the pregnancy at this early date ask how Jane is feeling, whether we are excited, if we are nervous. They congratulate us and tell us that we'll be wonderful parents. I know they mean it as a compliment, but right now it sounds like the pilot saying, "I'm sure the parachute will open" just as you jump out of the hatch. "How are you preparing?" is a different question altogether. It's not about the future; it is about this moment, this place, this spot where we are. It is about looking into the future, but from where we stand now.

How *are* we preparing? We are moving forward on the obvious things. We are diligently reading books about pregnancy and childbirth, learning what will happen as weeks turn into months and months turn into trimesters. We have begun to think about how to transform the spare bedroom into a nursery and where to stow the furniture that's in there now. We have visited one maternity clothing store, escaping just before Jane hyperventilated at the waistlines. We have made an exploratory trip into the utterly intimidating warehouse of Babies "R" Us, where I was made breathless by big-box babyness. Jane and I walked through the aisles, dwarfed by towering shelves of must-have baby items, while other expectant parents compiled their registries, shooting at items with handheld scanners that looked like radar guns.

I felt like I was in a foreign country. I had no notion how to go about choosing the right car seat. I didn't know when or, for that matter, why strollers became travel systems. I didn't know what we need to have or do to stimulate tactile learning, visual learning, and musical aptitude, but evidently we are supposed to do—and buy—something. I didn't know if we really need—or even want— to communicate with the baby *in utero*, but we found products to help us do this, as if Jane's belly were some sort of curvaceous Ouija board. I had no clue whether we'll need two bottles or twenty, and whether they should come from Avent, Gerber, Ansa, or Playtex. I didn't know whether we want to put dirty diapers in a Diaper Genie, a Diaper Dekor, a Neat System, a Diaper Champ, or a garbage bag. Maybe we should just use cloth. It seemed almost simpler. We even found a diaper wipe warmer that could be ours for only $22. That's where I drew the line.

"I'm sorry, but I am not warming this kid's wipes," I told Jane as we escaped from the store. "Baby's got to learn sometime that this is not a Warm Wipe World. It might as well be right away."

When Rebecca asks her question, I realize that in the midst of all the excitement and amazement, I also feel a certain sense of grief. Jane and I have been best friends and lovers for over eighteen years. Virtually all that time, we have been absorbed in each other, for better and for worse. We have been repeatedly told, by relatives, friends, and strangers, that we make a good team. Now, this nearly two-decade chapter of our lives is coming to a close. Of course there have been changes in our lives, but for years, our relationship has been the two of us walking together in the world. Now it will be the three of us. I am excited about the change, but there is a sorrow in it, too. Milestones are markers of how far you've come, but they are also signs of what has passed.

One thing we have done is figure out when we can expect the baby to join us. According to the online pregnancy calendar on Babycenter.com, a Web site that I check, oh, four or five times a day, our baby is due on or around March 19. I find this wholly, utterly, amazingly auspicious because it is the date, many years ago, when Jane and I first kissed.

It only took a few weeks after we met in college to fall fast and deep into love, but we spent a year and a half simultaneously reveling in it and denying it. While everyone else went on dates, got drunk at frat parties, or just got down to the business of having sex, Jane and I talked. We romanced each other with words, regularly keeping lists during our conversations of additional thoughts we wanted to share, lest one of them get washed away by the rushing current of words. Within a few months of meeting, we started a new campus newspaper to write down and share the things we were talking about. We had no editorial standards to speak of, beyond printing things that seemed interesting to us, so our paper ranged from feminist politics to intentional Christian communities to bad poetry to gay rights.

When we weren't talking to each other, or to the campus, we were writing letters. During school vacations, we sent each other thick, eight- and ten-page letters heavy with hyperbole and senti- ment. "Bernhard of Chartres once said that we stand on the shoul- ders of those who came before us to gain our view of history," Jane wrote in one of her near-daily letters during our first summer apart. "It is humbling and inspiring to realize that without the Emma Goldmans, the Celestes, the Eleanor Roosevelts, the Sarah Black- wells, the Heloises, the Hatshepsuts, and the Rita Mae Browns, there would be *no* inspiration. No aspirations. We stand on their shoulders, you and I and the women of our world who really can be anything they want to be.... We stand on their shoulders. No idea is ever mine alone. And I need never fear isolation. I need never fear historical loneliness."

I absorbed every letter from Jane like hungry summer soil sucks up rain. I responded with pages and pages that hopscotched from what I was thinking while reading Plato to my fantasies about start- ing ISIS, the International Sorority of Independent Sisters. I mused about whether heaven exists, listed some pros and more cons of capitalism, and speculated about how and why people change and how and why they don't.

We believed unfailingly in each other, and in doing so, we be- lieved in ourselves–that we were possibility incarnate—that the world was ours.

The summer after my freshman year, I rode a Greyhound bus to visit Jane at her home in Newburgh, Indiana. Situated on the northern bank of the Ohio River, Newburgh is a town of 3,100 peo- ple and more than 25 churches. Spotted with cornfields and horse farms when Jane was growing up, Newburgh has become a suburb of Evansville, Indiana, its residents feeding the work forces of Alcoa and Toyota. But still, its identity is small Southern river town. Newburgh is nominally above the Mason-Dixon Line, but in truth, it sits on the fence. The city trustees erected a plaque by the river commemorating July 18, 1862, when Newburgh was distinguished by becoming the first town north of the Mason-Dixon Line to be captured by Confederates in what Newburgh, like its Southern sisters, refers to as the War Between the States. The capture happened, the plaque notes, without the firing of a single shot. The Confederate crew just rowed across the river and snatched ammunition and supplies. The invaders never fired a shot because they had no shots to fire—their weapons were all decoys. There is no explanation of why no one in Newburgh waged a fight; maybe they were just as happy to join forces with Dixie. Even now, there are plenty of Rebel flags on the bumpers of trucks driving around town.

On the evening of my arrival, Jane introduced me to her girlfriend, Beth. I knew about Beth, and had known since the previous fall when Jane told me over a pot of tea in a practice room in the music building that she was a lesbian. At the time, I was less surprised by her revelation than by my own: if Jane can do it, so can I. Until that moment, despite several crushes on other girls and a passionate, inexplicable adolescent infatuation with Joanne Woodward, it had honestly never occurred to me that I might be gay. I just thought I was bad at dating.

Neither Jane nor Beth had told their families that they were lesbians, nor, for that matter, lovers, although most people had by that time drawn their own conclusions. Jane was working that summer as a hostess at Casa Gallardo, Evansville's misguided and short-lived Mexican chain restaurant, so while she was at work, Beth undertook the responsibility of entertaining me. She took me to a movie one night, out to dinner another. Beth was smart, funny, and more aware than either Jane or I of the threat that I posed. By the time of my visit, I had begun to identify myself (but only to myself) as bisexual, but the truth of the matter was that the only person of any gender who interested me was Jane.

Over burgers and fries, Beth told me how much she loved Jane and could never bear to lose her. She went on, in case this was not persuasive enough, to tell me earnestly that she believed Jane walked the line between genius and madness. Upset the relationship, she implied, and you just might tip Jane over the edge into dithering insanity. I listened, half aware of why she was lobbying me and half convinced that I would never allow myself, on principle, to become the Other Woman.

But in the moments when Beth was not there, I toppled further into love. Jane took me to her favorite places, a sort of informal tour of southern Indiana dreamers. We visited the Saint Meinrad Archabbey, a Benedictine community that has been praying and worshiping since the 1850s. We went to New Harmony, the site of two nineteenth-century utopian experiments that espoused communalism, industry, and education but ultimately disintegrated in the face of theological dissent, individualism, and decidedly unutopian malaria. We walked to the dam, where there was an overlook onto the Ohio River. There were no other people around, all chased inside by the chewy southern Indiana humidity. There were only butterflies, Monarchs, flashing orange in the sunlight. Arms outstretched, we stood in the grass while butterflies perched on our bodies, tickling our wrists and shoulders and foreheads.

At night, Jane came home from Casa Gallardo smelling like chimichangas. She showered, turned on some music, and we sat in our pajamas and talked into the darkness. One night, late in the week, she sat on the bed, wrapped in a red-and-white-striped robe. A candle burned on the nightstand. I lay next to her, looking at her face, her wet hair combed back, a few drops of water trickling down her cheeks. In that moment, I knew beyond question that I loved her. For the first time, I knew beyond any doubt that I could kiss her. But I didn't.

In the fall of my sophomore year, Jane went to Greece for a semester abroad. We wrote effusive letters about the books we were reading, campus politics, Delphic oracles, the sky above the beach at Crete, and drinking frappes on the plaza in Athens. After Jane's return, we were not just drunk on sentiment, but throbbingly, achingly hung over on it. We spent long dinners in the dormitory cafeteria, our feet entwined under the table, talking about anything and everything. We lay on Jane's bed, cuddling and holding hands. We ate all our meals together, walked to class together, spent every evening together.

We also drove each other nuts. We leaped easily to anger. We clung to each other and we pushed each other away. Meanwhile, Beth, the girlfriend-from-home, suddenly began appearing for regular visits, like a human wedge. I promised myself again and again that I would not cut in, but in fact, I already had. I was enraptured and jealous and tingling and wholly in love. We were a walking soap opera.

On the evening of March 19, Jane and I planned to get together as usual, to study and read and talk and touch, wittingly and unwittingly. But this night was different. I took the highly unusual step of primping, taking care to style my always-unruly hair as carefully as I could manage. I put on my favorite clothes: small yellow t-shirt, droopy pink cotton sweater, jeans. Jane had managed to procure a bottle of Polo Brindisi wine from the local IGA, a cheap red with just a hint of fizz. We had port wine cheese spread and a box of Wheat Thins. She put an album on the turntable, a singer from Greece who sang, I imagined, songs of love and honey.

We spread the burgundy-streaked cheese on our crackers and drank some wine. We talked about things I no longer remember, probably our classes and what we were reading. We talked about everything except what was about to happen. Finally, we stopped talking. I lay next to Jane, our arms around each other, our faces brushing, our breath mingling. I promised myself again that I would not kiss her. First. It was my compromise with ethics: I will make myself wholly available to be kissed by this person with another girlfriend, but I will not kiss her first. She stopped waiting. And in the moment of that kiss, there was a burst like an electrical jolt. We both felt it, a surge that ran the entire lengths of our bodies. Like lips long parted had finally found each other.

[V]

Jane is sleeping. Every day now, she crawls home from work and goes immediately to sleep, lying like a fallen soldier on the battle-field. She hauls herself up to wolf down a plate or two of food, then shuffles back to her pillows. She lies unmoving on the bed or the couch, our two cats sprawled blissfully on top of her. In these early weeks of gestation, she is all hormone, her breasts swelling, her energy sapped by a creature still smaller than a guppy.

Meanwhile, my inner guy is coming out of the closet. I feel urgently, irrationally protective of Jane. I want to stand guard over her, to protect her from drafts, from worry, from bacteria-laden soft cheese, from cat litter, from free-floating germs. I want to tell her what to do and what not to do. While she sleeps, I go outside and mow the lawn. I pull weeds in the garden. I turn the compost. I climb an aluminum ladder and clean the gutters. I sweat. I stink. I feel positively virile.

Is this the role of the nonbiological lesbian mom—to be a faux dad? Am I becoming a "DH," the "dear husband"—or designated hitter, for all I know—that all the straight women write about on the Internet discussion boards I visit? I don't feel like I somehow need to mimic the paternal role, but yet it seems to be finding and claiming me. I am a little worried that I am somehow fueling the stereotypes of right-wing complementarians who argue that every woman needs a man, every man a woman, and every child one of each, to have proper balance in the universe. Maybe major change inherently promotes traditionalism, a grasping for the models most familiar, if not necessarily the most fitting. Or maybe the experience of the unpregnant partner, whatever the gender, follows a predictable pattern. It's just that most of the unpregnant partners in the world are men.

When Jane is not sleeping, we go to the bookstore. We are both believers in the idea that reading bestows control. The trick is finding the right books. In the Pregnancy and Parenting section of the store, she settles down on a chair. There is a mound of books by her side, all explaining to expectant mothers in more or less exhaustive detail what is happening to their bodies, what they need to worry about, how to worry less, how to exercise, why they shouldn't exercise too much, and on and on.

Meanwhile, I find myself drawn to books for new fathers. Compared to the absolute onslaught of books for pregnant women, who apparently have nothing to do but read, there are surprisingly few volumes directed at men. Based on what I find, dads still seem to be remarkably marginal to the whole process of reproduction. The general pregnancy books mention men in an almost offhand way— as in, it's good to have Dad involved. Or, Dad can help with parenting by giving Baby a bottle. Many of the books actually targeted at men emphasize manliness: book jackets designed to look like men's clothing, "Guy's Guides" to the mysteries of pregnancy. They are gestational positioning devices, promising to help men navigate the wilderness of pregnancy.

None of these books expect men to be naturally good at much of anything relating to parenthood except, maybe, teaching the kid to throw a ball. They assume anxiety and a certain cluelessness, which may be why I find them consoling. Books for guys provide the most basic information, while books for Mom are far more sophisticated. While Dad learns how to keep from dropping the baby, Mom learns the various hypotheses about what causes colic, the dangers of strep B, and how to do yoga with an infant.

Finally, I buy a book for stay-at-home dads. I like the topics it covers: balancing child care and work, defining responsibilities for housework, developing shared family goals. We are actively discussing the prospect that I might quit my job and take care of the baby after it is born. After spending so much time and energy deciding whether to have a child, neither one of us wants to hand our baby over to a stranger, no matter how much more they might know than we do. Many of the questions faced by stay-at-home dads are also mine. Should I quit my job or work part-time? How will I feel about not earning money? Will it affect my self-esteem? How about my virility? How will I feel about being the principal caregiver of our child, but not the (biological) mom? How will Jane feel about going back to work and leaving our baby with me?

Thinking of myself as a dad, maybe a stay-at-home dad, feels a little safer than thinking of myself as a mom, especially when I'm not the one who is pregnant. Among the dads, I feel less anxious about becoming a parent. I realize that I have certain huge advantages over many men, at least the ones portrayed in the books and magazines directed at women. Female anatomy won't come as a shock to me. I know something about cramps. I've been up close and personal with a speculum. I believe completely in the earth-shattering power of the female hormone. I know how to run the dishwasher, oven, and washing machine, so I don't have to take a course in basic housekeeping. I don't need to be told to help occasionally with the grocery shopping. In contrast to these guys, I am positively prepared.

But if the truth be told, I feel more at home among the dads because I have never thought of myself as a particularly good woman. I have never regretted being female nor am I even remotely butch; I'm just not very good at girl stuff. At my favorite coffee shop, a young guy who works behind the counter frequently wears a t-shirt that reads, "You make me feel like a natural woman." Every time I see him, I want to hug him. If he feels like a natural woman, I think, there might be hope for me.

When I was a teenager, the things that girls were supposed to care about never really registered in my life. Like boys, for instance. I tried several times to have a boyfriend. A couple of them turned out to be gay. On the rare occasions that I was asked out on a date, I became painfully introverted and verbally inept, trying to guess what my lines were when I didn't even know what play we were in. My most successful relationship was with the boyfriend who lived in New Jersey. I lived in Ohio.

Mercifully, it never occurred to me that perhaps I was unsuccessful with boys because I was meant to look at girls. At the time, I would have been utterly unequipped to deal with the notion. I suppose the warning signs should have been obvious. Other girls developed crushes on Burt Reynolds. I had a thing for Kristy McNichol. Other girls loved the Bee Gees. My favorite band was Queen.

What does it mean to be a natural woman? I have no idea, but I am convinced that other women know. While I was trying to get pregnant, I went to a birthday party to which one of the guests brought her three-week-old daughter. When Baby entered the room, heads spun faster than Linda Blair's. Women clustered around the still puckery little girl whose sandy blond hair fell onto her forehead, whose tiny, dime-sized eyes were closed in sleep. Within seconds, a line formed to hold her. Most of the people at the party were lesbians who had no children of their own, although some were in the process of trying to get pregnant. As each person held the baby, someone else would invariably say to them, in a tone of coy innuendo, "You look really natural, there." Eventually, the baby was passed to me. I sat in an armchair, believing as I do that it is always best to sit down when holding an infant, in the same way that it's always best to wear gloves and a hat when facing a hazardous situation such as a dead bird on the porch. I tried not to move and barely breathed, convinced that she might suffer Sudden Infant Death Syndrome while lying in my arms. Eventually, as was bound to happen, someone looked at me and said, "You're looking really natural." Wink, wink. So does Astroturf, I thought. I certainly didn't feel natural. I felt fraught with danger. I was aware that at any moment, Pookie's head could fall off. She could become fatally overheated in her fleece receiving blanket. She could smother in her onesie.

I feel like a distant cousin to the natural woman. Maybe I would have felt even more unnatural as a pregnant woman. But still, I wanted to know what it would feel like to grow a baby. I wanted to know how it would feel to nurse. I wanted to know if I could give birth.

Now that Jane is pregnant, I acknowledge that I don't know what I'm doing, but not that I don't know what's best for her. I have granted myself the solemn responsibility of being Jane's protector, although some tiny part of me admits that she has not asked me to do this. I am bossy by temperament, an inclination that is growing in direct proportion to Jane's rising hormone levels. I shoot directions at her like telegrams. Do this. Stop. Do that. Stop. I want her to follow my directions because I am sure it will be good for both her and the baby. I could lighten up, I think. But I don't.

"Go take a nap," I tell Jane, for the fourth or fifth time today.

"I don't want to," she says.

"You seem tired."

"I'm fine."

"It would be good for you."

"I'm *fine*."

"OK. Whatever. It's just that you won't have as much time to sleep during the week. And I know how tired you were last week."

Jane glares at me. Her lips are pursed and tight. "You can't be so pushy about what I do or don't do, and what I eat or don't eat, and when I sleep or don't sleep." She goes on. "This is absolutely our baby, but it's *my* pregnancy."

She is lying on the sofa, covered with cats and sections of last Sunday's *New York Times*. I stand by the side of the coffee table as she talks, but inside, I'm running. I hate her anger, even more so when I suspect she's right. I dodge.

"I'm sorry," I say. "I didn't know I had upset you." This is bullshit. I know Jane well enough to know exactly when I am pushing her too hard. But I continued anyway for reasons that I do not fully understand. My eyes are stinging.

Don't cry, I think. Don't get angry. Don't look hurt. I tell myself that she has every right to say what she has said, every right to feel the way she does. I even partly believe this. I also know that repeating it to myself will throw a wet tarp on my own smoldering feelings. I come from a family that is largely clueless about how to deal with anger, especially among other family members. We've tried lots of approaches, from rage to denial to Valium. As for myself, I generally stick with passive aggression followed by retreat. Jane thinks we're all nuts.

It's not until the next morning, when I wake up exhausted and depressed, that I realize there might be something bigger going on. I find it impossible to focus on anything. I sit at my computer and obsessively browse the sections for dads on Babycenter.com. I don't know exactly what I am looking for, but I know that the sections for new moms do not apply to me. I am not pregnant. My breasts don't hurt. I don't throw up before breakfast. At the same time, as much as I might empathize with the men, the fact remains that I am fundamentally an outsider in the Dad sections. I don't know where I belong. I am in limbo between being a mom and not being a mom and being a dad and not being a dad.

The phone rings. It is Jane's mother. She asks how the mom-to-be is doing. I say she's doing great—pretty tired, but not too nauseous. "And how is the mom-to-be's, uhh, helper?" she asks. I know that she doesn't know what to say, what language to use for her lesbian daughter-in-law. I know this, but I feel as though I have just been shut out of the Mommy Room.

"Fine," I say slowly.

What and who am I? Mom? Dad? Mommy's Little Helper? What's my role here as the non-birth mother? And what is my role as a non-birth mother who tried to be a birth mother? Jane has asked me how I feel about not getting pregnant myself. A few other friends have also asked. Until now, I felt fine, but I have made a lifelong habit of the delayed emotional reaction.

When we visited the clinic for Jane's first pregnant-woman exam, the nurse—who had inseminated me several times—turned to me and asked: "Are you jealous?" I almost fell off my chair. Her question was not asked in an insensitive way. She was genuinely concerned, I think, that Jane's pregnancy might be hard for me. But it felt suddenly and intensely personal, an unexpected shift in focus from the details of Jane's body to the details of my psyche.

"Uh, no," I said. In that moment, I didn't feel jealous or angry or betrayed or any of the things that I could have been feeling about the fact that Jane was the one housing our zygote. But then again, maybe just a little.

"I would have liked to nurse," I said a moment later.

She explained to me that there are ways. I should call the La Leche League and talk to a lactation consultant. "You can just tell them that you're adopting, if you don't want to tell them your whole gig," she added. "Some women can stimulate milk flow. And there's also this tube that you can wear so the baby can have formula while sucking at your breast. You should try it."

Maybe, but then maybe not. I feel overwhelmed just thinking about it, as though it throws me ever deeper into a liminal space. I could be a semi-mom, non-dad who nurses. Gays and lesbians often say that we spend much of our lives making our own road maps. This feels to me a little too much like making the road.

I don't know how other lesbian, nonbiological mothers-to-be, who tried to get pregnant and could not, might experience their partners' pregnancy. For that matter, I don't really know other lesbian, nonbiological, presumably infertile, mothers-to-be. I don't even bother looking for books on the subject, which is just as well because, as I find out later, there aren't any.

It's my general impression that I should be in pain. I know that many women, straight and otherwise, go through a great deal of grieving when they try to get pregnant and can't. I have heard about other lesbian "non-birth moms" who feel resentful toward their pregnant partners, or bitter about the pregnancy. I don't think I feel that way. I am excited that we will be having a baby, but the excitement is tinged with some sadness. I feel left behind in unmarked territory. I am expecting a baby, but I am not pregnant. I will be a mother, but I won't have given birth. I will adopt our child legally, but my experience has little or nothing in common with most adoptive parents. There is really no category, no name for what I will be. I am defined by what I am not: a nonbiological parent, the non-birth mother.

I sit at the computer, my stomach clenched. Tears roll down my face and splatter the keyboard. I don't know what I am. I am a woman becoming a dad. Or something like that. I certainly had my own set of doubts about whether I would make a good parent, but unlike the guys I read about (most of them, anyway), I wanted to get pregnant. I am not mourning the loss of my pregnancy; I am mourning the absence of it. Now that we are settling into the rhythms of Jane's doctor visits and morning sickness and rising hormone levels, I am missing what never was.

As Jane moves from Herself to Herself Pregnant, I am increasingly an outsider. This is not because Jane is actively trying to exclude me, nor is it because I don't want to be involved. The reality is that she is undergoing something intensely and profoundly visceral and I am watching. When Jane first realized she was pregnant, we began to refer to our little zygote as "the Speck." "You're the Speck Jar," I teased her. "And I'm the Spectator," I added. It struck me as funny at the time, but it just seems sad now. To some extent, the Spectator is exactly what I am. I am involved, supportive, bossy, coaching, protective, but utterly outside.

Jane is becoming someone different from who she has always been. I am still myself, but wandering in new terrain. I feel a little ferocious about wanting to be part of this pregnancy, as though I am lashing myself to her leg to know what is going on, to feel some of what she feels. I don't want to let her go on without me. I don't want to be left behind.

A few nights later, I have my first baby dream. In it, Jane is pregnant, and so am I, and we are somehow carrying the same baby. Mine is a carbon copy of hers. We decide that I should have an abortion, so I go to the clinic, which is in a Target superstore. I ask a clerk where the clinic is. She has no idea, but she directs me to a bank of escalators. I ride up and down, up and down, looking for it.

[VI]

Early on a steamy Sunday morning in July, Jane comes out of the bathroom looking stricken. "There's some blood," she says. We have both read the section on miscarriages in our pregnancy book many times over and know that bleeding at this point in a pregnancy is bad. But how bad? We don't know.

"There's not a lot," she says. "But it's definitely there and it wasn't before." Her lips are pursed. "I may be having a miscarriage," she says and sits down heavily on the sofa next to me. Maybe she is. I don't know enough to have a sense of whether this spotting is normal, a fluke, harmless, or the beginning of the end of this pregnancy. What I do know is that we are at the peak of the miscarriage danger zone, Week Six. I know that the risk of pregnancy loss drops considerably after the eighth week. That seems impossibly far away.

I think about what I remember of the symptoms. Will Jane start bleeding or cramping? Will I need to take her to the hospital? How do I get to the hospital? Do people go to the hospital for miscarriages? I barely know. I go into the other room and check the directions, just in case.

Jane begins to cry. "I'm sorry," she says. "I feel like I must have done something wrong." I try to assure her that she hasn't done anything wrong. She has been doing everything right, in fact, with the possible exception of the doughnut-hole binge a couple of nights ago. But even a bucket of doughnut holes wouldn't cause a miscarriage. It happens—or it doesn't. And we don't even know what's happening, if anything is happening at all.

Nonetheless, a nagging fear tugs at me: have we unwittingly caused this? We went to a commitment ceremony yesterday for two friends, an exuberantly lesbian, two-and-a-half-hour affair at which friends and family shared their memories of and hopes for the two women celebrating their relationship, which is now in its tenth year. The ceremony was followed by a reception at a park shelter on an island in the Mississippi River. There was dancing and we joined in, despite the penetrating heat. As we were leaving, Jane got dizzy and so we sat by the river for a while, waiting for a breeze. Maybe we did too much. Maybe Jane got too hot, too tired. Maybe we did do something wrong.

I can taste my fear rising. If it wasn't the dancing, maybe something else is going on. Jane hasn't been very nauseous, I think. I know that a lack of morning sickness can correlate to a higher incidence of miscarriage. Is that a bad sign? She hasn't been quite as tired this past week as she was the week before. Is she somehow becoming unpregnant? Is the baby dissolving?

Jane looks at the enormous bouquet of pink and lavender and yellow flowers that my father sent us a few days before. "I hope we still have some reason for those," she says and begins to sob. I pull her toward me and kiss her hair. I feel her tears drop on my leg as my own run down my face.

At 7:23 a.m., Jane calls the doctor and leaves a message. After about half an hour, the doctor on call phones back. She is reassuring, saying that spotting does not necessarily mean that something terrible is happening. She asks about the color of the blood. It was brown. It might just be old blood, the doctor says. Maybe a small blood vessel broke and this blood just took a while to appear. It's not over till it's over, she reminds Jane. But just to be safe, she advises Jane to be sedentary for a day. No lifting, no exertion, no laundry, no grocery shopping. Jane settles in on the couch. The clock slows to a plod, dragging between minutes like a child walking toward certain punishment. We sit and look at each other.

There's nothing to do. I find it extraordinarily frustrating that pregnancy consists mostly of waiting. I want a plan, but the plan is only this: wait. It's not that I can't be patient. I have a high tolerance, and truthfully, a certain affection for deferred gratification. Even as a child, I regularly made up rules and rituals for waiting. I would save my favorite Halloween candy so long that it actually turned stale. I would eat ice cream in minute bites, smoothing over the surface after every tiny dip of the spoon. I would save money, not for any particular purpose, but just because I liked putting it in the bank. As I got older, I began writing plans and schedules, mapping out the course of the day, or the week, or the year. Jane is less in love with rigidity, but neither one of us leaps without looking. We are both thinkers and planners and waiters.

But waiting when you don't know what you're waiting for is another thing altogether. We do not know what is happening inside Jane's body. We have no way of gauging what may or may not be happening to the baby. This is the paradox of pregnancy: we are simultaneously consumed by skyrocketing expectations and yet utterly unable to know what to expect. Even if Jane is fine today, there is no way of knowing how things will turn out two or six or eight months from now. It occurs to me that there is never a way of knowing how the future will unfold, but I ignore the thought.

Meanwhile, Jane and I are silently, methodically conjuring our own lists of reasons why she might be having a miscarriage. I am calculating how fast I can get to the hospital. Jane is monitoring every flinch for possible cramping, every twinge for latent abdominal pain.

"We probably don't need to panic about this," she says after about thirty minutes.

"Right," I say, trying to sound convinced. Five more minutes plod by.

"We should learn from our friends who don't panic," she says. "Like Ed," a friend we know from church. "He falls off a ladder, smashes his wrist, manages to call an ambulance, and then makes sure to clean up all the blood before the emergency team gets there. Now, that's someone who doesn't panic."

This is not my way. At various points in my life, beginning with early adolescence, I have convinced myself that I had one life-threatening, or at least debilitating, illness or another: heart disease, a brain tumor, arthritis, cancer of the tailbone. Jane has her own neurotic variations. When she encounters illness, whether her own or someone else's, she goes almost immediately to the Internet, seeking out articles from the National Institutes of Health database, the *Journal of the American Medical Association* or *Gut, an International Journal of Gastroenterology and Hepatology.*

We limp through the day. Jane goes to the bathroom to check for more spotting every half hour or so. Meanwhile, I clean. Once the porch is vacuumed, the laundry done, the kitchen mopped, and the living room dusted, I begin to feel incrementally better. Jane has settled in to watch television, sitting on the futon in the spare bedroom. I am hoping that she will fall asleep. Television sports are like video Valium for her. Today she is watching golf, which I think is the athletic equivalent of a sedative on the best of days. I tiptoe down the hall and nudge the door open. She's wide awake.

"I can't sleep," she says. "I'm still worried."

I lie down on the couch next to her and the cat climbs on top of both of us. The cat is the only happy one here. I fall asleep in Jane's arms.

When I wake up, her eyes are still open. She goes to the bathroom again to check for blood. Still nothing. "Maybe it's going to be OK," she says tentatively.

The afternoon passes. I take the cat out for a leashed walk around the backyard. Jane finds a baseball game on television. I read for a while, then stop back to check on her. She is fast asleep, the soft music of America's pastime humming to her like a lullaby. I tiptoe to the side of the futon. This is the room that we plan to turn into a nursery. I can barely imagine what it will be like. I can barely imagine that Jane is pregnant, still, and will be tomorrow. I stretch a cotton blanket over her, pulling it around her hips and waist. I tuck her in.

[VII]

A few weeks later, Jane and I lie cuddled under another blanket, on the quilt-covered bed in the cabin we have rented on Madeline Island, one of the Apostle Islands in the fringes of Lake Superior's southern waters. Almost all the cabins on the island have been endowed with names. Ours is Hideaway, and it suits us perfectly. There is a nice kitchen, a deluxe edition of Scrabble, and no noise except for the constant splatter of rain on the roof. Surrounded by trees and overgrown brush, Hideaway is barely visible from the gravel road that cuts up the north end of the island. We lie in bed, wrapped in a comforter, and look through a scrim of trees at Lake Superior, the coldest, the deepest, and today, the wildest of the inland seas. Due to the ring of islands that make up the Apostle Chain, the water here is normally relatively calm, at least compared to the oceanic waves of the North Shore. But today, the wind has stirred the lake with giant beaters. The water froths against the land.

There's not much to do on Madeline Island, which is one of the reasons Jane and I return here each year. It's good for the occasional bear sighting, wading in the shallow water at Big Bay Beach, playing cards, and drinking cocoa. There's one good restaurant and a smattering of mediocre ones. There's the burnt-out bar that serves pizza and burgers as side dishes to beer under the remains of its burnt-out roof. There are our fantasies about buying a place here one day, although we both realize that we are thirty years too late to find anything even remotely affordable. There's even less to do when it's raining, which is what it has done almost the entire week that we have been here. We bundle up in sweatshirts, venture out to the coffee shop, play gin rummy, eat ice cream, cook the pork chops we brought from Minneapolis, and drink tea. For Jane, this is perfect. It's close to her ideal vacation anyway, and it matches exactly her sagging energy level as she reaches the end of her first trimester. In between bouts of doing nothing, she naps.

So a storm here is blockbuster entertainment. Earlier this morning, we drove into town, pulling up in front of the coffee shop that also serves as a wine store and gift boutique. The regulars—long-time vacationers and a handful of year-round residents—were talking about the storm. The sailboats tied up at the dock are going down, they said. Yup, that wind's pretty strong. Jane and I walked to the dock to take a look at the foaming water. Amazingly, the ferry was still running to the mainland and, even more amazingly, people were still riding it. The incoming ferry lurched to the dock like a boat on a pogo stick. We walked along the town's main street to a small beach off of which several sailboats were anchored, some of which were still upright. One man had tied the end of a rope to the dock and the other end around his waist. He was paddling a small rowboat out to his sailboat, which was lying nearly sideways on the water. What he expected to do when he got there was a mystery to me, but I admired him for trying.

Jane and I watched the sailboat rescue attempts for a while and then returned to our cabin. We ate some sandwiches and grapes, then crawled back into bed.

Now we watch the trees shake their branches in the wind. We watch the water stream down our bedroom windows. And we watch each other.

We have always been strongly focused on each other, and this pregnancy is making us even more so. Jane says she just wants to sit at home and grow a baby. I want to sit with her and watch. I suppose we are caught in the hormonal waves that direct one species or another to the nest-building of its own kind. I did not expect that I would be experiencing these desires as well, but I want little other than to hold and enfold her. We are preparing for change, and we turn toward each other. We intertwine.

We spend hours curled into each other, reading predictable mystery novels. We lie in bed and belt out songs from the 1970s and 1980s, in a sort of musical duel to lodge an annoying song permanently in the other person's head. Jane launches into the old Styx classic, "Come Sail Away." By the time the lads are ready to take off on the merchant sea, I have my revenge planned: John Denver.

I begin to sing "Rocky Mountain High." "You bitch," she says, laughing.

I hold Jane, her head heavy on my chest. I rub her back. I kiss her hair.

We are both aware that this is probably the last vacation that just the two of us will take. Even if we leave the baby with someone else in the future and slip away by ourselves, it won't just be us. There is both a sadness and a sweetness in this, a passing of one way of being and an entry into another. I want to hold on to each moment, remember her smell, memorize the weight of her head on my shoulder, study the deep brown of her eyes. Perhaps it is the latent historian in me that spurs this desire to archive experience. I want to savor what we have been or, more than that even, what we are right now. Babymaking returns us to the dreaming and hoping and believing that brought us together in the first place. Those were days filled with imagining what we could become. We are imagining again.

Even though our baby is, in many ways, still very much an idea, it has begun to have a presence and an identity in our lives. We have begun to make space for it in our home and in our imaginations. Is this what makes an embryo or a fetus into a baby, this imagining into being? It seems to me a more reasonable, if more ambiguous, measurement than viability or doctrinaire notions about person-hood beginning at conception. We are beginning to imagine the baby being with us, holding the baby, listening to the baby scream, watching the baby bounce on fat sausage legs. This is what makes the baby real and makes the baby ours. We are calling it into being and into an embrace.

Falling into a baby, now that we are doing it and not just think-ing about it, feels more and more to me like falling into love. At the beginning, it is all giddiness and uncertainty. Then, premature certainty, perhaps mixed with ambivalence. Then, sooner or later, free fall. My inclination is to move through life rationally—and I certainly spent a long time debating parenthood—but ultimately both Jane and this baby could become part of my life only through a leap between a known world and an unknown one. In both cases, lover and baby, there came a moment when I realized that I was no longer standing on the ground but instead, floating on air.

The sun finally emerges on the morning that we leave the island. We go to one of the local fruit farms on the mainland, high on a hill overlooking Lake Superior, and pick thirteen pounds of blueberries which seems to me, food hoarder that I am, barely sufficient. Then, we stop at a coffee shop in town and have steamed milk sweet with honey and vanilla. Adjoining the coffee shop is a toy store. We have not bought anything yet for the baby, in part because it still seems so early, and in part out of superstition that we might somehow jinx the pregnancy. But this is our week to stretch our legs over the abyss between just us and our family. We go into the toy store and pick out a small, floppy teddy bear, the size that an infant could clench. It's time to go home.

THREE

Segues

[I]

ON THE MORNING OF THE FIRST DAY of the thirteenth week of Jane's pregnancy, I walk into the living room. Jane is sitting on the floor surrounded by piles of mittens, scarves, and hats. After twelve weeks of dragging herself from naptime to nighttime, she is freakishly awake. It's seven-thirty on a warm Saturday morning in September and she's reorganizing the coat closet.

"I guess your hormones shifted," I say.

"Apparently," she says, sorting mittens. "Next, I'm going to mow the lawn."

This Jane is far more familiar to me than First Trimester Jane. This is my take-charge, organized, clear-thinking Jane. She is herself again, just fatter.

It is reassuring to have her back, but at the same time, I will miss the Jane of the past three months. She was dull, but she was wonderfully soft. She craved closeness and showed a sort of primal dependency that she normally does not indulge. We have always been emotionally and physically close, but during her first trimester, Jane wanted to be constantly by my side. She lay in bed with her head on my chest for hours, her body heavy and limp. Rather than protecting her own independence, she wanted to rely on me. Rather than being the resident nurturer, she wanted to be cared for.

Hormones are odd mind-twisters. The forces buffeting Jane's emotions were at least as strong as those reshaping her body. I found to my surprise that I was subject to them too, as though sucked into her powerful magnetic field. For three months, I had almost no desire to see other people or do other things. Lying in bed, with Jane's head on my chest, was thing enough.

Part of it was the smell. Maybe it was the estrogen soup cooking inside her as she grew a baby and a placenta, but she smelled distinctly different during the first three months of her pregnancy. I found it addictive. I wanted to bury my nose in her neck and gasp back her scent.

"What do I smell like?" she asked as I snuffled in her shoulder one morning.

"Like earth," I said. "Like musk. Like leaves. Like sex."

And she did. Her smell was irresistible. When I held her or when we kissed, all I really wanted was to breathe her in. Does this happen to other people? I haven't found it mentioned in the pregnancy books. Is it an evolutionary device to ensure that the pregnant woman will be protected and accompanied during the critical initial period of gestation? Is it a sort of natural perfume that the spouse is incapable of leaving?

Jane is more herself now, and smells like herself too. Now, instead of falling into my arms at night, she gives me a kiss and rolls over to read the *New Yorker.* Now, instead of sweet musk, she smells like Infusium shampoo and Dove soap. The spell has broken, and we are ourselves again, but waiting.

[11]

The phone rings. It is our friend, Mark, calling to say that he and Andrew want to talk to us about something. *Something.* Pregnant Jane is in no mood for mystery. "What is this something?" she asks. We almost know.

Years ago, when we had first moved to Minnesota, Andrew and Mark introduced us to some other friends with whom we've established an informal dinner club, meeting four or five times a year at one or another's home for a long evening of semi-gourmet eating. Last week, the dinner club got together. For the first time ever, Andrew didn't come. There was no explanation. We almost know.

One of the best things about the friendship that Jane and I have with Andrew and Mark is that it feels so organic. And yet, because I am a lesbian, I am sometimes unable to keep myself from second-guessing it. Compared to many of the lesbian couples we know, Andrew and Mark rarely talk about feelings. Do I like this friendship so much because it exempts me from really talking about my emotions? Am I taking refuge in guyness? Am I that dysfunctional? Lesbians, at least the ones we know, have a strong predisposition to be process junkies. We like to tell each other our "stories" in that monologue sort of way. Our get-togethers tilt surprisingly easily toward therapy. I know far more about some lesbians' history of depression and family-of-origin psychodramas than about what they do for a living. There is a weird, almost manufactured intimacy in the habit of telling each other our secrets before we tell each other our interests. With Andrew and Mark, we don't talk at length or with much intention about feelings or pain or dysfunction, or any of the other topics that so often seem to give lesbian conversations credibility, but by virtue of spending time together on a regular basis, we know what we need to know.

At least I think so.

"Andrew wants to break up," Mark tells Jane and Jane tells me. I feel the air being sucked out of me.

We make plans to go to their home that afternoon. It is, ironically enough, eight years to the day since Jane and I celebrated our own union ceremony. A framed picture from that day, of us standing next to Andrew and Mark, rests on the shelf in our living room. When we get to their house, Jane and I sit on the sofa. Andrew and Mark sit in armchairs at opposite ends of the small living room.

Andrew does most of the talking. He has been feeling unhappy for a long time, he says. His friends don't really understand him. We don't really understand him. He feels called to do something different with his life. He feels called to leave.

We almost knew, but we had no idea. Jane and I ask questions: Is he sure? Have they considered seeing a counselor? How can this be so sudden? Can't they work it out? Andrew becomes increasingly defensive, as though we are telling him that he cannot, should not, follow what he feels he must do. He says that it is his right to leave, which it is, and that he shouldn't be expected to stop just because it doesn't please us. He reiterates his points like a public relations spokesman trying to stay on message after a chemical spill.

Jane asks how they want us in their lives in the future. Mark immediately says that he definitely wants us to continue to be part of his life. Andrew says nothing.

After about forty-five minutes, we leave. There doesn't seem to be anything else to say.

The only divorce I have experienced intimately was my parents.' But that one, which was so long expected and which occurred after I had already been away at college for a year, feels remote compared to this. Andrew and Mark are not technically married, of course, so they are not technically divorcing. There is no procedure, no protocol. Andrew moves out of the home he has shared for years with Mark and just sort of disappears. It is as though he has vaporized. He is gone.

I feel like the ground has shifted under our feet. There is a gaping hole where we thought there was solidity. Jane and I have lost a vision of our future, the one we mused about with Mark and Andrew over pork roast and sweet potatoes, in which we would have a baby and they would adopt one, the one in which we would arrange our professional lives so that we could each spend a day doing child care, we would go on vacations together, and we would live together in

old age in adjoining apartments, our devoted children dropping by
to share meals and play board games.

It's an odd thing, in the gay community, that family is both
devalued and hypervalued. Because so many people have relationships with their biological families that are remote even on good
days, there is a tendency to write off family as a loss, part of the
price of coming out of the closet. It is certainly not true of everyone, but there are still many gay men and lesbians for whom
family is steeped in shame. Family gatherings are times of semi-
strangulation, when conversations are censored and partners are
studiously not invited. Parents still pray for their children's sal-
vation and send religious tracts in the mail. Plenty of people still
"straighten up" their homes before Mom and Dad come to visit—
removing pictures that are "too gay" or even purging all evidence
of an unacknowledged boyfriend or girlfriend—something they
would never think to do when gay or lesbian friends come over.

When the family is not accepting, it is relatively easy to con-
clude that family doesn't really matter. Family becomes something
to leave behind in Fargo or Trenton or Louisville, shaking the dust
of childhood soil off our feet. We trade family for "relationships,"
in the absence of anything more formal. Gay men and lesbians will
speak of being "in a relationship"—or not—far more frequently
than they will speak of their "relationship" as their family.

At the same time, family is prized. For all the fluidity of our "relationships," gay men and lesbians regularly form groups of friends
that go to extraordinary lengths to support each other in times of
need. There are plenty of examples of people ditching each other
when things get difficult, of course, but there are many other stories of friends nursing each other through illness, offering financial
support, or opening their homes to friends who are struggling. In
every Gay Pride march, the contingent of Parents and Friends of
Lesbians and Gays, populated by gray-haired moms and dads carry-

ing signs reading, "I love my gay son" or "I am proud of my lesbian daughter"—and, increasingly, by kids with signs saying "I love my Moms" or "I love my gay Dads"—receives a surge of heartrending cheers.

More than I had realized, Andrew and Mark were our family. Families change, of course. People change. People divorce; lives come together and then move apart. Is it any different for us than it is for straight couples, when their friends break up? I don't know. But I do think that there is something precious about finding family in the gay community. To much of the world, all of our relationships are "just friends." We are unrelated, untied to each other. Our families do not technically exist until they are documented on paper. There is no marker when our relationships end. We even struggle with language. Our spouses are "partners" or "girlfriends" or "boyfriends" or "lovers" or "significant others," all terms that are ultimately insufficient in one way or another. In the broader world, no one moves to be closer to their friends. No one quits a job to spend more time with their friends. It is the ties of family, the ties of blood and marriage, that are seen as irreversible, supposedly inescapable. But in our world, the lines between friend and family are blurred, making both simultaneously essential and extraneous.

Jane and I play and replay our final conversation with Andrew and Mark, trying to find some sliver of light that might illuminate why this has happened. Our mutual friends are equally confused. Several call us to ask what in the world is going on. We can hypothesize, but we cannot explain.

In the weeks that follow, we hold on to Mark and he holds on to us. We continue to have dinner once a week or more, Andrew's usual chair standing empty. I take to sitting on what was their side of the table, just to distract from the void. We cry. We listen to Mark's stories and his wrenching efforts to make sense of his loss. We try to figure it out. We never really do.

Jane responds like a wounded animal. She is angry, and even more than that, she is hurt. Both she and I had assumed the security of a future in which our baby would grow in a circle formed by the four of us. We had assumed the permanence of this family. Now, that vision lies in shards on the ground. Jane becomes fiercely protective of the baby, as though Andrew's departure has in some way threatened its safety. She curls inward, perhaps attempting to prevent her own pain from seeping through the umbilical cord and introducing the baby, far too soon, to the sour taste of sorrow. Cat-like and defensive, she guards the baby from hurt, shields it from loss.

[IIII]

We are going to look inside our baby. Because, at age thirty-seven, Jane is at elevated risk for bearing a child with Down syndrome, and because we are both at elevated risk for anxiety, we have decided to do a Level II ultrasound. A longer and more thorough exam than the quick scans done so far by the nurses at Jane's clinic, the Level II ultrasound doesn't just look inside the uterus, it looks inside the child. It is possible to view the fetal brain, the spine, the kidneys and liver, the four chambers of the heart. Our intention, officially, is to make sure that all the various body parts are developing as they should be. We will be looking for signs of genetic dysfunction: in particular, a thickening in the neck, short upper arm or thigh length, and, apparently, a crook on the pinky finger—all of which could be indicators of Down syndrome. Now that Jane is nineteen-and-a-half weeks into her pregnancy, it is unclear to both of us what we will do if the exam turns up a problem. What we really want is to be reassured.

Jane has known all along that her age automatically puts her pregnancy into the high-risk category. This annoys her, partly because she bristles at having any standardized definition applied to her, ever, and also because it is frightening. Far better to have the doctor tell you that everything will be fine than to hear, every time you go to the clinic, that you are high-risk.

It doesn't help matters that the women in Jane's family, who traditionally breed young, are obsessed with her age. Jane is the baby of the family by fourteen years, so she is surrounded by siblings who are approaching retirement, sending their kids off to college, and babysitting for grandchildren. When they found out about the pregnancy, both of Jane's sisters independently noted her advanced age. "Well, I guess it's OK," her oldest sister said to her on the phone. "After all, you look younger than you are."

Her mother is especially fixated on Jane's age, maybe because she was also thirty-seven when she became, quite unexpectedly, pregnant with Jane. In 1965, that really was high-risk. In addition, Jane was placenta previa, the ill-placed organ blocking her entrance into the world. Her mother began to hemorrhage in labor and Jane was delivered through an emergency C-section. There are reasons for her mother's angst.

Still, there is nothing to do about Jane's age and relatively little to do about her risk level. She has already cut out caffeine, reduced her sugar consumption, stopped drinking alcohol, given up cleaning the cats' litter boxes, stopped riding a bike, and quit eating any fish that might be high in contaminants. She doesn't smoke, do cocaine, sky dive, water ski, or ride horses, or she would give those up, too.

But because the medical establishment believes Jane to be high-risk, we have discussed at length whether or not she should have any of an array of tests to check the health and well-being of the fetus. The least invasive, the triple screen, is a blood test, taken around the sixteenth or seventeenth week of gestation, that measures the levels of proteins and hormones secreted by the fetus into Jane's bloodstream. It does not claim to diagnose anything, but it can provide some measure of whether the pregnancy is more or less risky. Depending on the levels of hormones and proteins found in the blood, the test can indicate whether the baby shows increased risk of Down syndrome, spina bifida, anencephaly, or a variety of other genetic conditions. The results, however, are far from conclusive; further, the test generates a high percentage of false positives. Of women whose blood shows abnormally high levels of the measured proteins, as many as 90 percent may be carrying babies who are, in fact, perfectly healthy. So what would the test tell us? Quite possibly nothing, but we hope it will give us a sense of our odds.

We also talked about doing an amniocentesis, which would provide much better information, especially in diagnosing Down syndrome. We shied away from it, however, both because it involves shooting a needle through Jane's abdomen and into her uterus, which struck me as a singularly bad idea, and because it can raise the risk of miscarriage. We gave even shorter consideration to chorionic villus sampling, in which the doctor would remove a bit of tissue attaching the pregnancy sac to the wall of the uterus. The test can be done much earlier—around week ten—but it can raise the chance of miscarriage to as high as 1 in 100.

We want to be reassured, but we do not want to endanger the baby. We want to know what to expect, but all we can really know is that we are expecting. The tests provide percentages and chances and likelihoods, but not one of them can tell us in advance what the baby will really be like. What would we do if we found out that the baby has Down syndrome? Cystic fibrosis? Spina bifida? We still would not know, really, what the child's capacities might be. Neither would we know how a genetic condition might affect a child's life span. Nor would we know whether the child would be in pain. For every prognosis, there are exceptions. What's more, we are aware that there are no guarantees that a child born healthy won't contract something a few years down the road. Cancer can't be predicted, nor accidents, nor bizarre viruses.

Is it better to know—and know what? Before she got pregnant,

Jane believed that there were conditions which, if diagnosed positively, would cause her to consider terminating the pregnancy, and
I agreed. Now, neither one of us is so sure.

In the end, we opted for the two least-invasive tests: the triple
screen and the Level II ultrasound. The triple screen results put
Jane at the low end of risk for her higher-risk age group. This was
good news, but vague, so we decided to proceed with the ultrasound
anyway. Because it actually looks at the baby—the inside of the
baby—we think that it might be able to give us more conclusive
information.

On the appointed day, we arrive at the clinic and are escorted
into the genetic counselor's office. The counselor, Suzanne, sits in
a swiveling office chair. She appears to be in her mid-forties and is
gentle-spoken, blond, calm. A quotation from the Buddha scrolls
across her computer screen. She takes out a clipboard and begins
to ask questions, filling in our answers on a chart with a series of
circles and squares to represent different members of our future
child's family tree.

Suzanne asks Jane pleasantly about her family history. How
many siblings? Three. Is everyone still alive? Yes. How old were
various family members when they gave birth? Much younger than
we are. Are there any birth defects or congenital conditions in the
immediate family or their offspring? No.

"Now, how about the father?" she continues.

"The donor," Jane says. "He's in good health, except for some
allergies, according to the sperm bank." That's about all we can say
because we have stupidly arrived without the health history that we
printed out from the sperm bank's Web site. I try to remember the
specifics, but all I can recall for certain is that he is Lutheran.

We tell Suzanne that Jane carries the gene for cystic fibrosis, a
genetic tidbit that we learned only after she became pregnant. We
also learned that a surprising number of people, especially Cauca-

sians, carry one of the genes that causes the disease—about one in twenty people. When we found out, I immediately called the sperm bank and spoke with a doctor who assured me that, yes, the bank screens its donors for the thirty most common genetic mutations that lead to cystic fibrosis and, no, it does not accept any donors who carry them.

"The thirty most common mutations?" I repeated into the phone.

"Oh, well, there are hundreds more, but they're rare," he said. "We don't test for those."

When I relay this information to Suzanne, she seems annoyingly unconcerned. We are apparently lower risk than we thought. I watch to see if she codes our chart with any other little shapes, maybe miniature curlicues for Overly Concerned and Somewhat Neurotic. I begin to wonder if we should even be here, if elevated age really means elevated risk. Based on Suzanne's reactions to Jane's answers, I am beginning to think that Jane still has several good breeding years in her. Suddenly, I think about siblings.

"I'll go tell the technician that you're ready," Suzanne says, with a pleasant smile. A few minutes later, we are led into the sonography room where Jane is instructed to climb up onto the exam table, hike up her blouse, and drop her skirt below her hips. The sonographer squeezes thick green gel, like slimy toothpaste, onto her belly. I sit in a chair by the wall. We both watch a screen on the opposite wall where the scene inside Jane's body is projected.

The sonographer is systematic and efficient. "I start at the top and work down," she tells us. She immediately pans in on the brain. Two hemispheres appear on the screen, full and even. With one hand, she moves the transducer like a computer mouse over Jane's abdomen, smearing the goo. With the other hand, she types rapidly on her keyboard, printing out photographs of our baby's body parts like ticker tape.

She examines the neck. Everything looks normal, she says. That's a good sign. She moves the transducer around to get a better view of the face. The baby has one hand over its mouth, which annoys the sonographer, who is trying to get a look at the lip. Finally, the baby's head moves. The lip is fine. She moves on, first to the neck and then the spine, which looks like an unfastened bracelet stretched across the screen. The heart does indeed have four chambers. Blue and red shapes flash on the screen. Apparently the blood is going in the right direction. Two kidneys. A liver. All good.

She drops to the pelvis. "It's a girl," the sonographer announces in a matter of fact voice. She types: G-I-R-L, the letters showing up on the screen, appropriately enough, between the baby's legs.

I am reeling. Suddenly, there is a person in this baby: a girl, a daughter. There is a difference of vast magnitude between having "a baby" and having "a daughter." I stare at the murky picture projected on the screen. I feel protective in a way that I have never felt before. This is our daughter. I want to wrap my arms around her, guard her from danger, protect her from harm.

A resident comes into the exam room and stands on the side, watching. When the sonographer finishes, finally, at the toes, which check out fine, the resident takes over at the controls. She is pleasant enough, but pregnant herself and clearly tired. After the sonographer leaves the room, the resident moves the transducer aimlessly across Jane's abdomen, printing out a picture here and there. She chats blandly about her own pregnancy. Fifteen minutes go by.

Finally, the attending doctor comes in to review the results of the ultrasound with us. He says that he has looked at the pictures taken by the sonographer and everything looks good. He says that he will just check to make sure nothing got overlooked.

"Have you been practicing good ultrasound habits?" he asks the resident.

"I think so," she says half-heartedly.

He steps into didactic mode. "You should always start at the top and work down," he says. He proceeds to repeat the entire ultrasound exam, pointing out blood flow and umbilical cord, checking and rechecking the work that the sonographer has already done.

I am getting anxious. I don't know why the doctor is repeating the exam when he has already reviewed the pictures. I don't know why this moment needs to be a Lesson in Sonography for the captive resident. I don't know why he is still pushing the transducer across Jane's uterus. I don't know why this is dragging on for an hour. I don't know if this is hurting the baby.

"She's turning away," the doctor says, frustrated. He chases her, his slippery opponent, as though tracking the German submarines for which ultrasound technology was first developed. He checks the projected weight of the baby. "About twelve ounces," he says. He looks at her limbs and head size. "Everything looks normal," he notes. "Arms are a little long."

I look at the clock. I don't know if I should tell him to stop. I don't know how he will react or what Jane would want me to do. I want this to end. I want to go home.

Instead, I sit in my chair.

Eventually, after an extended instruction to the resident on proper exam protocol, the doctor finishes. I want him out. He hands Jane some tissues and tells her that everything looks like it's within normal parameters. Jane cleans herself off and we leave the doctor's office, clutching the four pictures that the sonographer cut from the much longer strip and gave to us. They remind me of scenes from a dream: hazy, indistinct, unearthly. Our baby looks like she is surrounded by static, as though she is floating inside an old black and white television tuned to a channel it barely receives. The baby's face looks misshapen and a little demonic. The eye sockets look dark and empty. Her toes and fingers shine with a white glow. Her arms, however, look just fine.

In the hall, Jane begins to feel dizzy. We return to the waiting room and she sits down for a few minutes. She still isn't feeling well, so we decide to drive to a nearby coffee shop for a cup of tea.

Drinking my tea, I am angry and upset with myself for not intervening, for not cutting in and telling the doctor that enough was enough. I am worried that I have put Jane and possibly our baby at risk. I am upset that I didn't have the confidence to step in despite my concerns.

"It's really OK," Jane says, although she is unhappy, too. We are both pleased to have done the procedure and to know that all signs are good. Jane reminds me that ultrasound is considered a non-invasive procedure and it beats the hell out of the other options. But I think about a barrage of pulsing sound coursing through the water that surrounds our daughter. I don't want doctors messing with our baby anymore. I don't want tests for the sake of tests anymore. I want Jane and our child left alone to grow in peace.

[IV]

A few weeks later, Jane and I walk into the hospital's education room for our first childbirth class. Several other women are already here, all enormously pregnant, propped precariously on folding chairs and looking like bulging pods about to burst. It occurs to me, once again, that maybe I was just a bit overeager, signing us up when Jane is just in her sixth month. We find two seats and stow under them the blanket and pillows that we were asked to bring. Around us, women elevate their ankles. Some are rubbing their bellies. One woman is shoveling a supersize pack of McDonald's french fries into her mouth. Their husbands sit next to them, some looking engaged and interested, others about to bolt.

I feel like I'm wearing a name tag reading, "Hi, I'm Amie and I'm a Lesbian." We have entered heterosexual space. Until now, much of our experience with babymaking has occurred in the privacy of our home or a doctor's office, or has had some degree of connection to the gay community. But not this. If reproduction has traditionally defined the culmination of the straight experience, the childbirth education class is graduation practice.

I am not exactly worried that we will encounter outright disapproval. We chose this hospital in part because of its support for a variety of relationships: its maternity registration forms even have lines for Spouse/Partner rather than Husband. And presumably, the other couples are more concerned with how they're going to get their own babies out into the world than with whether or not there are lesbians in the room. Still, I feel like we stand out, as though two of these things are not like the others, two of these things just don't belong.

Then a lesbian couple we know walks in. We knew they were expecting, but had no idea they would be here. Even though we are only casual friends, I almost hug them. Just having them here makes me feel more like we belong in this place, like birthing is not always and only a straight thing.

We go over to say hello. The birth mom, who is very nearly the size of a mobile home, is from Kentucky. I ask her how she's feeling. "Like a pickled pea," she grimaces. "I go out and everyone stares at my belly. I mean, HELLO! Person up here." Jane laughs, half sympathetic and half relieved, I think, to have her own feelings voiced.

Now at six months, Jane has just recently entered the stage where her pregnancy is obvious and unquestionable—and, correspondingly, the stage where she feels like a Pregnant Woman first and herself second. Although Jane likes being pregnant far more than she ever anticipated, she would like it more if she could do it on her own terms. It annoys her that she is hungry all the time. It aggravates her that she has to leave meetings to go to the bathroom. It bugs her that getting out of the car is becoming cumbersome. It offends her that she is not allowed to lift and move heavy items whenever she wants to. It drives her crazy to have to ask for help.

Pregnancy slaps you in the face with the knowledge that much of who we are is defined by our bodies. On a daily basis, Jane is becoming less self-sufficient. Her growing stomach limits the clothes she can wear, the things she can reach, and the spaces she can fit into. Hormones course through her veins like hallucinogenic drugs, making her drop things, forget what she is saying in the middle of a sentence, and gag whenever she tries to brush her teeth. Her body is hot and tired and beginning to swell. And now she is surrounded by a room full of even hotter, more exhausted, and more swollen women, like perverse Ghosts of Christmas Future, presenting vision upon vision of what she will become.

At six o'clock, Katie and Angela, the class instructors, introduce themselves and welcome the Moms-to-Be and the Husbands-and-Partners. Smiling brightly, they tell us the number of children they each have (five and one). They are both nurses and certified childbirth educators. Both are thin and fit and extremely upbeat. Angela begins by holding up large placards showing the inside of a woman's body. First, she walks around the room holding a diagram of a non-pregnant woman. The intestines nestle cozily against the abdominal wall. The lungs look robust and expansive. The bladder is a small, comfortable balloon. Then she shows us pictures of the body at various stages of pregnancy. The organs shift and smash together, until, at thirty-four weeks, the lungs have been downsized and the intestines are pressed up disturbingly high against the back. "So, husbands and partners," Angela says, "you can see why Mom might be having more trouble breathing and why her appetite might drop off by the end of pregnancy. Because there's nowhere for the air and the food to go." The pregnant women in the room nod, their suffering validated.

Katie takes over. She walks us briskly through the major stages of labor—early labor, active labor, transitional labor, and pushing—promising to revisit each in more detail later in the evening. Then she holds up a maroon-and-white knit pouch. A plastic doll is stuffed inside. It looks like some kind of sadistic Home Ec project. Katie holds the loaded pouch in the air and, slowly, pulls the wool back and then pushes it forward, demonstrating what the uterus does as it expels the baby. A knit, tubelike neck serves as the vaginal canal. "You can see that the baby comes forward and then retracts a little bit," she says. "It's two steps forward, one step back." Jane sighs.

After a while of this to and fro, the baby crowns, and the pouch's knits and purls stretch around its plastic head. "At this point, you'll want to push," Katie says. "You won't feel pain as much as sustained pressure." The doll's head emerges and Katie shows us how the baby turns, instinctively, onto its side to ease the shoulders through the pelvis. Finally, the doll is born, and its knit umbilical cord, which has come disconnected, hangs limply from the pouch. But Katie is not finished. "Now you will push out the placenta," she says. She contracts the pouch again from the back and out pops a large burgundy stuffed placenta. "It's about the size of a dinner plate," she adds. "I want you to know that because when I had my first baby and the placenta came out, my husband thought I had pushed out my liver."

At the end of three hours, after we have discussed the various stages of labor and divided into small groups to play a game aimed at helping us discern the difference between early, active, and false labor, it's time for a breathing and relaxation exercise. Husbands-and-Partners are directed to move all the chairs to the side of the room. All the couples spread blankets and pillows on the floor and lie down. Katie dims the lights and turns on some New Age music.

"I swear to God, if you play that music while I'm in labor, I'll have to kill you," Jane whispers to me. Katie instructs us to close our eyes, and then she leads all of us through some relaxation techniques and deep breathing.

"Husbands-and-Partners," Katie says, "take a look at Mom so that you know what she looks like relaxed." Jane lies with her head on the pillow, the corners of her mouth drooping slightly, her eyes shut. Katie leads us through more breathing, some deep and full, some shallow and short, but always relaxed. Here, in the semidarkness, this moment feels intimate. Some of the husbands lean over their wives, rubbing their abdomens and stroking their heads. It is rare that I am overtly affectionate with Jane in heterosexual environments, and I realize that I am holding back. I want to cuddle up next to Jane, kiss her neck, and sniff her hair. I want to hold her close to me and float together on our breath. Instead, I simply lie behind her, my hand reaching over her side and resting on her belly. But even though I am holding back, I also feel a sense of safety and inclusion. We are here for the same reason as everyone else: to learn how to bring a baby into the world. I am lying beside my Jane, I am holding her, and, in this moment, this is where we belong.

[V]

Now that we know we are having a girl, we are actively considering what to name her. In truth, we have been discussing this for years, settling first on Robin, then Sarah, flirting with Renate, and crossing Lindsay off the list after Jane's niece nabbed it for her daughter first. We go on walks around a nearby lake and pull names out of the air.

"How about Laura?" I ask.

"It's OK," Jane says. We discard names that have too much alliteration; we both like Molly, but Molly Miller virtually ensures that we will have a child who cannot pronounce her *L*'s.

We have decided that the baby, whoever she is, will have Jane's last name. This is in part because I think that the person who carries the baby should have dibs on naming it. And it's in part because my last name, Klempnauer, is unwieldy at best. I'd like to tuck it into the baby's name somewhere, if a name like that can be tucked, but not in a way that she actually has to use it—or, more to the point, spell it—on a daily basis. I do have a certain fondness for my name and the bond it represents with a small and inevitably related group of people in Ohio, Missouri, Texas, California, and Germany who all share its clunkiness. But I have also spent my entire life saddled with annoying nicknames: Klumpy, for example, leaps to mind. And I have spent years correcting other people's mispronunciations of my name and have seen it turned into Klemtnauer, Clubflower, Klempenheimer, and Clint Miller. I have spelled it and spelled it and spelled it: K-L-E-M-as-in-Mary-P-as-in-Peter-N-as-in-Nancy-A-U-E-R. I don't feel a need to pass it on.

Jane, for her part, has suffered the curse of the generic. She constantly tries to dress up her name to differentiate herself, to distinguish her brand. We thought for a while about combining the two names, maybe as Milnauer, but we never quite got around to it. Hyphenating the two would result in a sixteen-letter surname, which seems out of the question. I toy with changing my name to Miller, but for the time being, I decide to stick with what I've got.

And then Jane says, "How about Hannah? I've always liked that name." It's a name I have never considered. I don't know any Hannahs. I have neither connection nor baggage with it. Over the next few days, I consider it. Hannah Miller. Hannah Klempnauer Miller. It seems to work, but I think it falls a little flat. Eventually, we dress it up a little more: Hannah Elisabeth Klempnauer Miller. We both like it. Hannah, this will be your name. Hannah, we are calling you.

[VI]

The next week, we return to the hospital for another round of childbirth training. Katie and Angela, perky as ever, tell us that the evening will feature a video of labor and birth. The video, which is sponsored by Pampers, features laboring Paula and her narrator husband. We watch as Paula begins to move into the early stages of labor. She walks around her home and talks about being excited and nervous. Then things take a turn. Paula begins to recognize that this is serious. She is in pain. After a while, she seeks relief in the shower, the hot water pulsing on her abdomen and back. From outside the door, we hear, "Oh, this is *wonderful*." Her husband tells the audience, "The shower really worked for Paula. Then we ran out of hot water."

Paula and Husband go to the hospital. Paula's labor continues to advance along the cycle that we have been studying, and we watch her move into the active phase. She is patently miserable. The nurses coach her, encourage her to keep breathing, reassure her that she can do it. Paula begins to lose hope. Eventually, she makes it to the last phase of labor, the time to push. She is hunched over, her face scrunched in pain and concentration. Her baby appears and slips away, teasing her, his head crowning and retreating. Finally, he slides out of her body and they place him, wet and red and slippery, on her chest. Paula is crying. I am crying. I sit in the dark in the education room, tears rolling down my face. I had expected to be frightened by the birth video, but instead, I want to see more.

After class, Jane and I walk to the car. She is quiet. "That video was so beautiful," I say.

"*Beautiful!!!!???*" Jane barks. "There was nothing *beautiful* about it." She looks stricken, as though a vindictive and cackling judge has assigned her a merciless sentence for a crime she didn't commit. "I can't believe that I have to do that," she says. "I just can't believe it."

A few days later, on Sunday morning, Jane tells me that she couldn't sleep, so she got up and wrote a letter to Hannah. "I wrote to her about fear," she says. "And how she doesn't have to be afraid."

"That's a good thing to do," I say. "I think it's good for Hannah and it's good for you."

We have decided to go to church this morning, which is an anomaly in itself, so we get ourselves ready. While Jane is finishing, I sit on the sofa in the living room and wait for her. One of the baby books we have been given, filled with sweeping watercolor illustrations of mother animals and their young, is on the coffee table. I notice that Jane has stuck some notebook pages in the back of the book. I pick up the book. "This book has such beautiful pictures," I say as Jane comes into the living room.

"You're not reading my letter to Hannah, are you?" she asks.

I am immediately testy. "No. I'm not reading it."

"Well, you have to admit that you have a track record," she continues. "You have to take responsibility for that."

She's right. I do have a track record. I have twice been sucked in by the urge to read a couple of pages of her journal. But that was years ago, I think, and I also was slapped upside the head by the ill luck of reading pages that she wrote when she was angry at me. Why did I go back a second time? To find something better, maybe?

"I took responsibility for that years ago," I say, my voice low.

She looks at me as though I am a stranger who has broken into her house, popped open a beer, and stretched out on her sofa.

"I don't know why you're so angry," she says. "You did it more than once. It wasn't years ago."

I become literal in moments like this one. I want dates.

"When was it, then?" I ask.

"I don't know exactly when," she says. "Contrary to what you seem to think, I don't keep a log."

I doubt that.

Changing the topic, if only slightly and in a passive aggressive way, strikes me as a good idea. "You don't have to go to church today, you know," I say.

"I don't think you want me to go. I don't even know what you want. Why don't you make that clear?"

Fine, I think, let's regroup. Take a breath. Reorganize the moment.

"Do you want to talk?" I ask.

"I'm trying to," she says, as she goes to the closet and pulls out her coat. She puts it on, followed by a scarf. She turns and looks at me.

"I don't think you understand," she says.

"What don't I understand?"

She grimaces. "You don't understand that your experience is different from mine. You don't understand that what I write and what I feel are private."

"I didn't read your letter," I say again. I feel pushed against a wall, all escape routes blocked. "I didn't read it and I'm not going to read it unless you want me to." And, I think, maybe not even then. So there.

She starts to say something else and I cut in to defend my innocence.

She looks up suddenly. "Shut up!" she yells. "Just shut up and let me finish. My experience is different and it's private and I can't trust you not to read what I write. I can't trust you."

She sits in the rocking chair in her coat and scarf. I sit on the ledge of the fireplace. My hands are shoved in my pockets. I pinch my thigh through the pocket of my jeans.

The tears burn my eyes. I don't really want to talk, although I feel a perverse compulsion to continue to do so. I don't want to tell her how much this hurts me. I certainly don't want to tell her that I understand that at least some of this is the pregnancy speaking, but

that what she has said has wounded me. How much of this is hormone, and how much is her? Seventy/thirty? Sixty/forty? I have
no way of knowing. I am having trouble seeing through the fog.
Jane is rarely angry in this way. I don't know what to say. Anything I say may just make things worse, may come back at me at a
later point: Yes, but you did read my journal. Yes, but you do get
depressed. Yes, but you are unpredictable. Is she not trusting me or
am I not trusting her? Can we hear each other at all?

I am angry, but more than that, I am sad. I am sad that she has
said that she cannot (or will not) trust me, that I can't be closer
to this pregnancy, that I can't be inside it. I am afraid that I may
perpetually be outside the pregnancy and childbirth and even the
parenting experience—The One Who Doesn't Get It, Who Cannot
Be Trusted. More than that, the One Who Is Outside.

That afternoon, we talk again, tentatively at first, as though laying our fingers on a still hot burner. "I am just so freaked out about
birth," Jane says. "I can't believe I have to do that. I can't *believe* I
have to do that. There has to be some other way."

"You can absolutely do it," I say. "I know you can. And we have
a good hospital and a good doctor."

This is really making no difference whatsoever.

"Did you see that woman's face in the video?" Jane asks. "I almost had to leave the room, my anxiety level was so high."

This seems like a bad time to bring up the whole birth-is-
beautiful thing again.

"Oh, Minxy," I say. "You're going to be fine. You're going to
be safe and I'll be there with you and experienced nurses will be
there with you."

"It'll be OK?" she asks.

"Absolutely."

She looks profoundly unconvinced, but willing to indulge me
for trying.

The next day, when Jane comes home from work, she announces that she hijacked the department meeting to ask the women around the table about giving birth.

"The department director asked if anyone had any burning questions, and I said, 'Yes. How am I going to survive birth?' All the moms in the room looked at me and said, 'It's called an epidural.' They also told me that the whole process probably isn't going to take longer than twenty-four hours. I can manage for twenty-four hours," Jane says.

She looks as though she can breathe again. She has received reassurance from women who, unlike me, know whereof they speak. She has been given permission to be afraid and also to accept help. There is a special authority in what these women say because they are so ordinary: work colleagues, not superheroes. They survived birth, so she can too.

[VII]

We go to yet another class, this one on how to breastfeed. The class is held in an auditorium-style room at the hospital. The instructors seem to have stepped out of a traveling show called "Up With Breasts." Although none of us would be here if we weren't pretty much committed to at least trying to nurse, the instructors remind us in a hundred different ways that "breast is best." They hand us a packet of information with diagrams of the breast's interior; pictures of proper and improper latches, the baby's mouth adequately—or inadequately—engulfing the mother's nipple and areola; and pages of information about the multitudinous advantages enjoyed by breastfed babies over their deprived peers. Among other things, we learn that breastfed babies experience many fewer illnesses and allergies, have fewer ear infections, are less likely to contract cancer, and save their happy families up to $1,000 per year in formula costs. We learn that breastfeeding promotes a strong bond between mother and child, enhances the baby's emotional development, and even promotes a healthier workforce. Choosing not to nurse, it would appear, is not just self-centered, but quite possibly unpatriotic. Nursing can be a little tricky at first, we are told, but once mastered, the milk will flow, the baby will grow, and all will be right with the world.

The instructors tell us about the all-important colostrum, the yellowish milkshake that emerges from the breasts in the early hours after birth. Thick and rich, it is chock-full of immunity boosters. Then we learn about foremilk and hindmilk. The first is sweet and tasty, designed to catch Baby's interest and entice her to keep sucking. The second is the hearty stuff, full of fat to help the baby put on pounds. We learn that it is important to fully drain one breast at each feeding so that the infant gets both foremilk and hindmilk. If mom switches breasts too frequently, say, every ten minutes as our mothers were advised to do, the baby never gets the fat-filled hindmilk. I wonder again how any of us survived.

Next, the instructors talk about how pain medications used during birth may slow the suckling instinct at first, but they probably don't cause lasting harm. *Probably*. To drive their passive-aggressive point home, they show us a blurry video of a groggy baby, spawn of a woman who selfishly put her own interests first and used an epidural. The baby looks lethargic, apparently too sleepy to root around for Mom's breast. But then, we also find out that babies don't really need to eat when they are first born—since they've been well-fed and well-kept for the past nine months. But then again, the instructors inform us, it's important to get that breast firmly lodged into Baby's mouth as soon as possible, so the little one starts to get the idea.

After a short break, it's time to learn about the various positions for nursing. The instructors tell all the pregnant moms to get a doll or a stuffed bear from the shelf at the back of the room. Jane, who is planning to birth a human, chooses a doll. Most of the dolls are pretty worn. Ours has plastic eyes that flip open and shut, but only alternately, in a sort of satanic wink. Her plastic arms are beginning to detach from her cloth body. But she's still better than some of the all-plastic dolls that lie like statues in other moms' arms. And then there are the bears.

The instructors begin with the clutch hold, noting that it's sometimes called the football hold. This seems to amuse several of the guys in the room. Mom is instructed to hold the baby along her arm at her side, as though running for the goal line. We learn about lifting the breast to get the right angle and encouraging Baby to latch on tightly. We shift to the cradle hold, the most conventional way of holding a baby, across the body, in the crook of the arms. "Be sure that your baby's ear, hip, and ankle are all in a straight line," the instructor says. Jane moves the doll across her body and nudges it half-heartedly into position. It's getting late and Jane is looking tired and bored as she pretends to nurse her doll. Clutch hold. Switch. Cradle hold.

This goes on for some time, as the future mothers practice their technique and as Husbands-and-Partners are invited to try it out, too. Finally, Jane leans over and rests her head on my shoulder. Her voice slips into Okie.

"What if your name is Rose of Sharon and you've got a homeless man in a barn?" she murmurs.

I start to laugh.

"No, really, I want to know. Clutch or cradle?"

[VIII]

We are warming up to the third trimester, which apparently means that this baby is really going to come. Which means that someone will need to take care of her. In the years that we spent planning a child rather than raising one, Jane and I agreed that we didn't want to go through all the exertions required to have a baby and then fork the kid over to someone else for eight hours a day. I don't want to become the women I work with, caught in what seems to be the destiny of the middle-class, educated, professional demographic: racing through the mornings to get the kids dropped off at day care, maintaining a full-time, high-powered career, hurrying home, picking up the kids on the way, and then cramming in an hour of Quality Time, goddammit, before bedtime. I tell Jane about my coworker who was upset for an entire day because her regular grocery store rearranged its stock. "I don't have time for this!" she moaned. This is not the life I'm hoping for.

Plus, there's the gay thing. I feel a desire to be extra protective of our baby, to create a world for her, at least for a while, in which families come in all shapes and sizes and configurations. I would like to teach her that it is not just political correctness to say that gay families are normal and good. I would like her to learn that she can be anything and anyone she wants to be. I think that we could find a day care option that is gay-friendly, but I wonder if that is enough. I would like Hannah to feel, at least for a while, that her family is not the exception. On some level, I think that we can transmit these messages better than anyone else, no matter how inclusive they are trying to be. Eventually, we sidle up to the decision that I will stay home with the baby.

Which sounds great, except that I have no real idea of what it might mean to be a stay-at-home mom. Will I find parenting exhilarating or maddening? Will I lose my mind? My self-esteem? Will I find it somehow liberating? Will I watch my brain sink into the diaper pail? I know there are lots of stay-at-home moms these days, but my mental model is stuck on Nickelodeon. I imagine myself the lesbian June Cleaver.

"So," I ask Jane one night, "are you going to expect me to meet you each evening at the door, holding a martini and inquiring sweetly how your day was?"

"Mmm, that sounds nice," she says.

I was afraid of that.

The truth is, in addition to wanting to be present for our baby, I have an ulterior motive. I have been looking for a career transition and it seems as though a baby will be just the ticket. I have been working in development (euphemism for fundraising) for the past twelve years. I got into the field, not because I intended to or even because I have any particular talent at asking people for money, but because, after living for four years in New York City, I was pretty nearly convinced that the end of the world was upon us, whether by global warming, ozone depletion, or asphyxiation by concrete. I wanted to save the world, and working for an environmental organization seemed like a good start. After sending out a raft of letters and working for one horrible year as an administrative assistant in a cancer research lab, a job I accepted when my bank account was hovering around $200, I got hired in the fundraising office of a national environmental group. Twelve years and four organizations later, I'm ready for a change.

That said, I am not someone who particularly likes segues. I want out of my job, but I am not sure what I want to do once the door is open. Do I want to be a full-time mom? Do I want to freelance? Do I want to do something completely different, but at the moment unspecified? Do I want to be a barista?

What I do know is that I am bored and disheartened by my job. I am tired of sitting at the computer every day cranking out grant proposals. I am sick of meetings that tread the same ground, stepping over and over in the same footprints. I am inclined to think that there is something out there that I am meant to do, although I'm darned if I know just what. I am inclined to think in terms of calling and vocation, which comes of growing up in a clergy family, I think, but it does not do me the favor of telling me what the vocation is. I know that I regularly feel trapped by my job, as though I am stuck in an office as a sort of endless penance. Working freelance looks appealing, in large part because I think it will be more flexible. Then again, I have never done it, so I cannot say for sure. For that matter, I have never done motherhood, so I can't say anything certain about that, either.

The ambiguity drives me nuts. I want to know where I'm going and what will happen when I get there. I assume that I will continue to work in some fashion, but I don't know what that fashion will be. On the one hand, I crave the structure and the clarity of a conventional, full-time job. On the other hand, the thought makes my stomach churn. The challenge is the segue: moving from one thing to another thing that is not yet there.

How do you become something new?

I sit at my desk while I am supposed to be writing yet another grant proposal and, instead, revisit my ongoing fantasy about Life with Baby. I imagine what our days will be like. I will take care of her, offering stimulating experiences (but, of course, never television). I will relieve Jane of the responsibilities of grocery shopping, going to Target, and cleaning the house. Being a modern mother, I will build a freelance career during naptime and do yard work on weekends. I will bake fresh muffins in the morning. I will have dinner ready when Jane comes home.

In the back of my mind, though, is the goading sense that if I am not working for pay, I will therefore be slacking. Although Jane and I both acknowledge that she has more career ambition than I do, I feel bad for even considering the notion of sending her back to the trenches while I spend my day reciting nursery rhymes and making bottles. Her income is significantly better than mine, but I feel guilty for dropping out of the income pool. We have discussed and discussed and discussed yet again our reasons for having me stay home with the baby, at least for a while, and we both agree that it is what we want. But it feels illicit to want it for myself as well as for the baby. The truth is that I want to be a full-time mom in part because I think it will be best for our baby and our family and in part because I no longer want my job. Is this legitimate? I feel like I am ditching my responsibilities.

So I turn to my book about stay-at-home dads to try to understand how they work it out. I notice in passing that the author urges stay-at-home men and their spouses to develop clear plans in advance about how they will divide the household chores and shepherd their time. It strongly encourages them to write a family mission statement and job descriptions for each parent, outlining their specific tasks and expectations. Jane and I talk briefly about doing this, but we never quite get around to it. Good thing we're such excellent communicators, I think.

Meanwhile, I still have a job, which means that I still have obligations to show up at the annual holiday party. Jane and I agreed years ago that neither of us would be obliged to go to the other's work parties, so I arrive at the appointed time, alone, while Jane elevates her ankles at home. I polish off a glass of mediocre chardonnay while I wait for the roving waiter to bring the tray of hors d'oeuvres within grabbing range. Across the room I see Kristine, who joined our staff about three months ago. I don't have much of a relationship with her yet because we work mostly on different projects. But we have been together in weekly meetings and, recently, a full-day retreat. She is chatting with someone I find funny and easy to talk to, so I go over to mingle.

Kristine is middle-aged and exuberant, an extrovert's extrovert. We say the usual hellos and murmurings about what a nice event this is. And then Kristine turns and looks me up and down.

"I have to say, you look just wonderful," she says.

I am surprised, though I do think I look rather dashing in my wool turtleneck sweater and black pants.

"Thank you."

"And you're having a baby in just a couple of months," she adds.

Oh, wow. Not unless I'm carrying it in my purse.

"I'm not pregnant," I say. "My partner is pregnant."

"Ohhhh," she replies with her bullhorn of a voice. "You're a womanlover. I *love* that!"

I have absolutely no idea how to respond. Mostly, Jane and I get positive reactions to the news of her pregnancy, but I have certainly never gotten anything like this. True, I'm out at work and feel perfectly comfortable talking about Jane. Everyone knows that I am a lesbian—at least everyone but Kristine—but do I really want them to think that I'm a *womanlover?* It's an odd choice of words, to be sure. But what bothers me, I think, is that it feels exhibitionistic, as though the sheets have been thrown back, right here between the cheese puffs and the stuffed mushrooms.

That night, after the party, I perch on the edge of the bed where Jane has snuggled in with a historical novel about Scotland, and tell her the story. She curls into fits of laughter. "Did you tell her that all the womanlovers moved to wimmin's land in 1974?" she asks.

In the morning, Jane gets ready for work. After breakfast, she puts together her cache of food for the day: a large grocery bag holding a slab of leftover spinach lasagna, two oranges, a banana, some yogurt, a bagel, and a bottle of water. When she's ready to leave, she gives me a kiss.

"Good-bye, womanlover," she says with a suggestive wink and pouty lips. "Have a good day."

[IX]

Day by day, night by night, Jane slides further into pregnancy and we slide further into waiting. Outside, an icy blanket of snow covers the ground. The cold winds slither under the doors and around the windows. Our furnace lumbers away in the basement. If heat rises, it must all be in the top two feet of our rooms, because it is emphatically cold here on the living-room sofa. At eight o'clock, it seems too early to go to bed, so we sit on the couch, reading. Jane is shrouded in a blanket. She has a chill.

"Do you want me to make you a cup of tea?" I ask.

"No." She rearranges the cat like a hot water bottle next to her bulging stomach.

"Would you drink one if I made it for you?" Some people say lesbians have a tendency to be codependent. I don't know where they got that idea.

"No."

"It would warm you up."

"*No,*" Jane says again. "You don't understand. It makes me pee every fifteen minutes. At eleven o'clock, I get up to pee. At eleven-thirty, I get up to pee. At eleven forty-five, I get up to pee again and I pray that my tiny bladder is finally empty. At midnight, I get up to pee and I start to think I have a chronic disease."

"And at two a.m.," I add, "you shake me and ask, 'Are you awake? Because I'm pretty sure I have diabetes.'"

She pulls the blanket more tightly around herself, snuggles the cat, and grunts. We forget the tea.

FOUR

Mise en Garde

[1]

"WHAT WAS THAT?" Jane taps me on the shoulder.

"What?"

"That sound."

It's 2:00 a.m.

"I didn't hear anything," I say. Of course I didn't. I was asleep.

"There was a thud. It came from the back of the house. I can't believe you didn't hear it."

I pull myself out of bed and do a circuit of the house. I have no idea what I would do if I ever found something or someone. Throw a slipper? Nothing looks unusual except that one neighbor has all the lights on. I come back to bed.

"Everything's fine," I say. I turn off the light.

Five minutes pass.

"I can't sleep," Jane says.

Pause.

"I'm hungry," she says.

"Go get something to eat."

"No."

Pause.

"I'm restless," she says.

"Go in the other room and read."

"No. It's cold in there."

She's right. It is. And it's warm in bed, where we should be sleeping. But I'm awake now.

"You want me to go make you a bowl of cereal, don't you?" I say. "You want to prop yourself up on pillows and eat it in bed while you read the *Smithsonian*."

"No," she says. "That would be selfish."

I see where I went awry.

"You want me to go into the kitchen and make two bowls of cereal, so that we could both sit in bed, eating them and reading."

"Oh, that would be nice," she says.

I roll over, pull up the blankets, and close my eyes.

In the morning, I wake to *Morning Edition*. Within the span of about fifteen minutes, I hear reports about a possible military strike on Iraq and South Korea's preparations for a "worst-case scenario" in its conflict with North Korea. We may not have burglars or raccoons prowling our house at night, but the news increasingly feels malicious, like an intruder intent upon harm. For the past few months, it seems, all we hear is the monotone drumbeat of impending war. In the moments when the news reports are not about war, they seem to be about something else equally dismal: water shortages, untamable viruses, the ever-present threat that clear blue skies might burst suddenly into flame.

Jane and I get up. We eat bowls of oatmeal, brown sugar, and raisins for breakfast. The voices of public radio drone on in the background, their calm, informed, and devastating tones reviewing the evidence for weapons of mass destruction hidden somewhere in bunkers under the soil of Iraq. I try not to listen. When Jane is gone, I sit at my desk and stare at the computer. I need to get to work. I have grant proposals to write, deadlines to meet. There's a special irony to the fact that I raise money for a news broadcast when I really can't stand to listen to the news. I should be busily at work, writing about how important it is for Americans to be informed about what's going on in the world. I should be writing about how information is a critical requisite for democracy. Instead, I stare at the blank screen. What are we getting into? I wonder what kind of world Jane and I are about to give our daughter. My hands lie limp on the keyboard.

Security is a scarce commodity these days, though maybe it always has been. It's nothing new that armies go to war or that markets tank or that people threaten each other. But it feels to me as though we are teetering on the edge of precipitous change. I don't know exactly what it is or how it will play out. I don't know if our nation will go to war and if we should or shouldn't. I don't know what it will mean that glaciers are melting and oceans rising. I don't know if I can trust the future.

Every parenting book I read, every video I watch drives home the point that a sense of security and protection is essential to the well-being of a baby and a child. It's critical for the young child to know that she can rely on the parents, that the parents will be there and will respond to the child's needs. During our childbirth classes, we watched a video showing a mother smiling and cooing at her baby. The baby responded with a fixed and focused stare. The mother then stared blankly at the same baby, her face inert and depressed, and the child became agitated, disoriented, distressed. Babies need to know that they are moving forward into a world where someone is waiting for them, where someone will protect them, where someone will welcome them. I think Jane and I can offer a sense of security to our child, but can we protect her from a dangerous world?

The news is foreboding enough. But then, the parenting magazines I browse and the advice books I read add to the endless warnings, listing for us the world's hazards. Weapons of mass destruction rarely make the list, but hot dogs do (choking), as does sleep (Sudden Infant Death Syndrome), cups of tea (burns), and basements (radon). The equipment that we buy for the baby also warns of danger. I have taken on most of the work of putting together the assemble-it-yourself supplies we are purchasing for Hannah, which is surprising because of my appalling lack of mechanical skill. But so far, I've managed to piece together the stroller and the bouncy seat and the crib. I follow the directions religiously, worried that a mistake might mean irreparable harm to our baby. "WARNING," the high-chair manual screeches, "Failure to follow these instructions could result in serious injury or death." "PREVENT DROWNING!" the plastic-baby-bathtub manual advises, which strikes me as a good idea. The manual for the bouncy seat we have been given warns that it can cause strangulation or suffocation. The manual accompanying the baby monitor we have been given reminds us, "This product cannot replace responsible adult supervision." On thirteen of its thirty-two pages, the stroller manual warns us in English, Spanish, and French that our baby will be at risk in one way or another if we do not follow the manufacturer's extensive directions. Our home, which I had thought was a reasonably safe place, is apparently a minefield of risk.

What's more, just as we are about to have a baby, Minnesota's legislators are arguing again about the state's human rights bill, several of them lobbying to remove sexual orientation from the list of protected categories. The most recent version of the bill went into effect in August 1993, the very week, in fact, that Jane and I arrived in Minnesota from New York. It seemed karmic. We chose to move to Minnesota in part because we wanted a good place to be gay. We had met in rural Indiana, which is resoundingly not a good place to be gay, and then lived together in New York City, which is quite good, but so exhausting that it almost doesn't matter. Then we drove our U-Haul across the Minnesota line just as the lawmakers cut the ribbon on the new human rights legislation. At the time, only eight other states included sexual orientation as a protected category. Now that the self-appointed family protectorate has picked up the goal of revising the legislation, we may find ourselves again an unprotected category. I have downloaded a copy of the bill with its proposed edits. Every time the words "sexual orientation" appear, they are struck out with a solid black line.

I wonder again if we can keep our baby safe. I have known for a long time that the law is generally not on the side of the gay person, but until now it has been a back-of-the-mind sort of consciousness. I have generally felt secure and have largely lived in protective circles, working for liberal-minded nonprofits, surrounding myself with people who are either gay themselves or unconcerned that I am. Even now, while we live in a 1950s suburban rambler, we have managed to find a neighborhood that has a long history of gay and lesbian residents. No one here seems fazed by our presence.

But there are rumblings. Letters to the editor in the newspaper shout at each other about homosexual marriage. Some of our legislators foresee the breakdown of the state should gay marriage come to pass. Advocates for the traditional family predict dismal fates for children who are deprived of one mother and one father. Increasingly, I feel a need to have a Plan B. Should we be thinking about an exit strategy? Do I need to learn the words to "O, Canada"? I am not sure how to measure threat because it almost always seems clearest in hindsight.

And now, we are about to bring a baby into post–9/11 America, at just the time when our president may or may not be leading us into war, as troops are massing on the borders of Iraq, as people have finally begun to really acknowledge that global warming is real, as we have had virtually no rain or snow—in Minnesota—from October to January. Maybe, I think, our timing was a little off.

What should I be doing? Should I go to Washington to protest? Stand vigil on the Lake Street Bridge, where Women Against Mili-

tary Madness hold their poster boards for peace every week? Write
to my congressperson? Pray?

For now, I turn to the Internet. I type "Hope" into the Google
search engine and get more than 425 million results. I find information on hope for cancer patients, hope for survivors of sexual abuse,
and Hope Worldwide, a charity whose mission is to bring hope to
a hurting world. These are good people doing good work, but it
seems to me that their efforts are necessary mainly because so many
people wound each other so badly.

On New Year's Eve, Jane and I went out for Indian food, which
is a semi-tradition of ours. At the next table was an Indian family
with a baby girl, maybe seven or eight months old, seated in a high
chair. She was happily playing with crackers while her family ate
their naan and *makhni*. Every now and again, a customer or a waiter
would walk by and say hello to her. Then an older woman from
another table came over and knelt down next to the high chair. She
held out her finger for the little girl to hold. "It's a New Year's gift
to see you," she cooed. "Yes, it is. It's a New Year's gift."

Although it feels almost unbearably trite, it occurs to me that
the world could use more beauty. It's not that the problems of the
world will be solved by cute babies and puppies, but somehow, it
seems important to grow beauty. Hope needs to be cultivated or it
withers. There are so many opportunities to be depressed, so many
objectively good reasons to throw in the towel. But there is also
something insistently hopeful about a baby, as though there must
be a reason for faith. As though, beyond the headlines, beyond the
screeching about weapons and war and lockstep morality, this is far
too fine a world to give up.

[11]

In a few days I will announce my plan to leave my job after Hannah is born. I am planning to take some time off after her birth
and then go back for four weeks. Then that will be it. The voice in

the back of my head is congratulatory. I've been fantasizing about breaking away from office jobs for about eight years now. I want to move toward freelancing. I want to do more writing. I want to stay home with our baby. But then there's the other voice, the one saying: "Are you fucking nuts?" The one that reads a litany of reasons why this is a bad decision: the limp economy, my inexperience with babies, the possibility that I'll never really write anything, the possibility of failure.

The fact is that now it has to happen; we don't have any other day care option and the baby will be here soon. For better or worse, she is a catalyst.

Having put ourselves in the path of pregnancy, we now stand squarely in the path of parenthood. There is less ambiguity this time, which I find disturbingly unreassuring. Before, we weren't sure that one of us would get pregnant, but now, it's pretty clear that we will be parents, and soon. What was once both an act of faith and an act of release now feels like neither. It feels more like anxiety—excitement, yes—but anxiety. I have no idea what parenthood will really be like or whether I'll like it or whether I'll be any good at it. I don't know if I'll become a freelancer or if I'll be back in a day job in a year or two. I don't know if I'll manage to become a writer. I don't know what it will be like to be a family instead of a couple. I don't know what it will be like to be a mother. Yet, here we are, in the path of parenthood and the path of change, and both are barreling at us, full throttle. We will find out.

[I I I]

In the meantime, I want to have sex. This is a little unusual in itself, since my sex drive is notoriously lackluster. I like sex, but I also like pot roast. For years, I have found it difficult to answer whether I would rather have sex or a really good meal. Both are nice, and they go well together, but there are many times when I think my stomach would win.

Jane's pregnancy has changed all that. I have found her irresistible, myself insatiable. Ever since she got pregnant, I have seen Jane as ripening, earthy, musky, curvaceous, delicious. Jane, on the other hand, especially in recent weeks, has experienced herself as progressively more exhausted, fat, swollen, awkward. Still, I am drawn to her body. I want to hold her, pet her, sniff her, lick her, kiss her.

For the first seven months of her pregnancy, as long as she has been awake enough to do it, we loved sex. While my libido has typically been slow to warm, it was revved by gestation. For the most part, Jane reveled in it, her body pumped up on hormones, its sensitivity hiked up to high volume.

We have consulted our pregnancy books about sex, of course, although I have failed to find anything that addresses our situation. The books say that it's possible to have sex pretty much up to the time of delivery. It might be possible, but it is not realistic. As soon as we reached the eighth month, both of us were too afraid of stimulating early labor to do much more than hold hands.

But tonight, I reconsider. I don't know if my visceral attraction to Jane's body will continue after she gives birth or not. Maybe I should be making hay while the sun shines. I climb into bed next to Jane.

"I feel like my pelvis is breaking," Jane groans as she repositions herself on her stack of pillows.

So much for tonight.

The next day, as we are chopping onions and garlic and boiling noodles for dinner, Jane tells me that she had a Larissa encounter. Larissa is a Russian immigrant coworker who has a history of asking Jane questions that are blunt to the point of rudeness by American standards, but quite possibly surprisingly discreet by Russian standards.

"She cornered me in the kitchen at work and asked how the pregnancy is going. I told her it was fine, that the baby's growing well and that I'm feeling good for the most part. Then she got very concerned and asked me, 'The pregnancy, the hormones, will it change your sexual orientation?'"

I choke.

"Hmm," Jane says. "I told her that wasn't really likely to happen. Then she said, 'Oh, good, good. Would be terrible shame for Amie.'"

[IV]

Jane has entered Month Nine, the final zone. She is tired and unhappy. Her ankles and calves are like water balloons. She is an overpumped ball. She spends most of the time when she is not at work sitting on the sofa, watching television, with her feet propped up on pillows. Every so often, she jolts backward. "The baby is head-banging me," she grimaces. "Think of a battering ram going at your cervix. From the inside." She sleeps only fitfully at night, so we have given up on trying to sleep together. Her nose bleeds regularly. She is phlegmy. She has hemorrhoids. "Everything on the inside of me is doing its damnedest to get to the outside," she says.

I, on the other hand, feel a disconnection from the impending birth and certainly from the pains and bothers that accompany it. And completely unlike Jane, I feel disconnected from the baby. I think of Hannah more as Jane's baby. Jane's body enfolds her. I am experiencing pregnancy only secondhand. I imagine the moments after birth, when the nurse will give the baby to Jane and say, "Here is your daughter." Intellectually, I know that she will be my daughter, too, but emotionally, my attachment still needs to be knitted. Jane's bond is already woven tight. Is this how fathers feel? I feel like maternal instinct, whatever that is, should apply to me too, should already have bound me to this baby, but the truth is that she is still a stranger to me.

Standing at the cusp of parenthood, I feel myself dragging my heels. Will I like it? Will I like the baby? Will she like me? How will this change my relationship with Jane? Will parenthood be like having a permanent houseguest? Who will I be?

Before she got pregnant, Jane worried about losing her sense of self. I understood her concern intellectually, but not really emotionally. I'm starting to get it now. Will motherhood fundamentally change who I am? Do I want it to? I look at Jane and think that pregnancy, at least, has not exactly changed her. More to the point, it has shifted her. She is herself and not herself. She is herself but facing in a new direction. She has segued.

As for me, I am encased in anxiety. My emotions are taut. I have begun to cry. A lot. I feel pumped up on hormones, but they are not my own. While I'm working, the usual little frustrations tip me over the edge into tears. I don't want to start weeping in the staff meeting, but I almost don't care. I have lost all interest in my job. I need to be elsewhere.

Meanwhile, Jane is experiencing what seem to be the pains of prelabor. This could go on for days. Or weeks. It's impossible to say. I start to cry just thinking about it. I feel a strong need to put the house in order, which is how I usually deal with powerful emotion. Jane feels a strong need to lie on the couch with her feet up. We have heard that one sign of impending labor is a whirlwind of activity by the pregnant woman.

"I don't think that the whole Merry Maid thing is going to happen to you," I say.

"Nope," she says with a grin as she readjusts the blanket across her lap. "It's happening to you."

So it seems. I have stocked the freezer with turkey enchiladas, navy bean soup, vegetarian chili, spinach lasagna, pasta casserole, sausage and pasta soup, and forty-one turkey meatballs. I add up the number of meals that I have reliably covered: only sixteen. I should make more.

I am concerned that the downstairs bathroom needs a cleaning and that my favorite jeans need to be washed. I have unpacked and repacked the bag that Jane has prepared to take to the hospital. I am concerned that her toiletries aren't packed yet.

"I'm *using* them," Jane says.

I notice that the watch with the good second hand has a dead battery. This is bad. I should get it fixed. I wash a package of Target diapers to use as burp cloths and stack them neatly on the changing table. I remember that I haven't screwed the changing pad to the back of the table yet. I have to get on that. We have been getting ready for the baby for months, of course. For most of those months, I still felt like I had time. And then I didn't. I am anxious, nervous, and urgently wanting to prepare. Most of what can be done has been done, but I am certain there must be more.

Jane and I recognized years ago that she is, by nature and temperament, pretty much a calico cat. She believes in her right to be comfortable, is smart and willful, loves to be petted, and hates to be told what to do. I, on the other hand, am clearly a dog. I love structure, require regular walks, am deeply loyal, and believe that however I feel right now is how I will always feel. And I worry. I spend a disturbing amount of time thinking about what kind of dog I am: brown, with floppy ears, with a dash of golden retriever.

I worry about things that could happen in the future and things that didn't happen in the past but might have. I worry about doing things right and doing things wrong. I make up horrible scenarios that involve freak illnesses, say, or being stranded on a mountaintop, and worry about how I would respond to them. I wake up worried, just coming out of a dream in which Jane has received a special fellowship to study overseas for a year and I am worried that she will leave me behind with the baby. "But it's a Saltieri Fellowship," she says in the dream. "I can't say no." When I wake, she assures me that she has never heard of a Saltieri Fellowship; that she is going nowhere; and that even if she did, she'd take us along. But, I wonder, would we want to go?

Through it all I worry about whether I can be a mother and wonder how disturbed I should feel that my sense of my own maternalism comes largely from cats. I lie in bed thinking about Mr. Saltieri, while Murphy, my little black cat with the three patches of white dotting his belly like ellipses, curls in my arm. He spends every night here, purring and drooling. He soaks up affection like a drippy sponge. Our other cat, Louise, is balled up next to Jane, purring like a lawnmower. Murphy's purr sounds more like a low idle. His whiskers tickle my face, and I tilt my head away. He reaches out a paw and gently rubs it on my cheek. I feel positively maternal. It's odd, I know. I do recognize that he is not my baby. He's not even my species. But I feel attached to him in a protective, parental sort of way.

Holding Murphy, I try to imagine what it will be like to feel Hannah in my arms. I want to hold her in the night. I want to rock her and feel her move. I want to smell her and listen to her cry. I want to have the physical relationship with Hannah that Jane has had for the past nine months, albeit in an external form. I want to cuddle Hannah and whisper to her, things she needs to know: "You are my very best girl. I will always take care of you."

Murphy scoots closer to my neck, lifts his lemon-sized head, and licks my cheek, dribbling slobber down my chin. The moment is lost.

Wiping my face, I wonder if this might just be a realistic prediction of what I am in for. I will hold the baby, feeling dreamily full of love. And then she'll vomit on me.

This is the mystery and the wonder of parental love, I think. It's not one-way; the child loves the parent just as the parent loves the child. But it is about need. Children absorb love. Loved children expect to be loved; they assume it in the same way that they assume the presence of air. Love the child and the child may vomit on you. The child may scream inconsolably. The child may have no more sense than a meatball. But love the child because the child needs it in the same way that a garden needs the sun. And the sun shines down on the garden purely because the garden is there.

[V]

On the Ides of March, a day that certainly calls for being on guard, Jane and I both begin maternity leave. This seems a little strange because there is still no baby. We are as prepared as Girl Scouts, even though Jane was kicked out of Campfire Girls and I never broke the Brownie barrier. The nursery stands ready to receive a baby. The list of phone numbers is printed out. The changing pad is screwed tight to the changing table. The music that Jane wants played during her labor is selected and packed. This is the week we will meet Hannah. Will it be tomorrow? The next day? We don't know, but we do know that by the end of the week, we will be parents.

In the morning, we go to the clinic for Jane's weekly status check. Given the fact that she has been having Braxton-Hicks contractions for the past couple of weeks, we think that the time for birth must be very near, any minute even. Whenever Jane winces or walks up or down a set of stairs, I expect her to burst into full-fledged contractions. I prepare to hurl our personal effects into the car and drive to the hospital at a moment's notice. At the clinic, Jane's usual doctor is not available, so one of his colleagues substitutes for him. She measures Jane, inside and out. "You're starting to efface," she says calmly. "And you're almost one centimeter dilated." I am incredibly disappointed. That's *it*?

We return home to sit on the sofa and wait. Meanwhile, the country is pulling on its army boots, donning its helmets and flak jackets, getting ready for war. President Bush will address the nation this evening and is expected to lay out an ultimatum for Saddam Hussein. We will be at war soon. Will it be tomorrow? The next day? It feels as though the nation is careening down an un-marked highway, throttle open, brakes defunct. I don't know if the government is doing the right thing or not. I don't know if Iraq is a threat to us or not. I only know that I am completely absorbed with impending birth and that there are people in Iraq who also are wait-ing breathlessly for their first child. Beyond that, I don't know.

And so we rent *Blue Crush*. It's a surfer chick movie filled with seventh-grade dialogue and gorgeous blond surfer girls in tiny bathing suits riding giant waves. We never watch this kind of movie. Our home video collection consists of about ten tapes of PBS documentaries on topics like Tourette's syndrome and Alzheimer's disease. Tonight, *Blue Crush* is a relief. There are no threats of war, no talk about weapons of mass destruction, no fears of dictators and terrorists and bombs. There isn't much of anything, really, except cute girls and a script that consists mainly of "Whoa, big one!" and "Bitchin'!"

Jane and I sit on the couch, watch the girls surf, and wait. This is what we do now. Time has slowed. It drags its heels, loafs and lingers. We are focused nearly entirely on waiting for birth. It is as though the universe has contracted to a chrysalis in which we lie, listening to three heartbeats, waiting for the moment to emerge.

One of Jane's coworkers, who knows about things like alter-native medicine and touchpoints, suggested to Jane that I rub her Achilles tendon to stimulate labor. We sit on the fat blue couch in the basement watching the surfer girl heroine face her fear of drowning and ride out to meet the giant wave. Jane's bare, swollen feet rest in my lap. She is propped against a pillar of pillows. I rub her heels. About halfway through the movie, Jane hauls herself up to go to the bathroom. I pause the film, mid-wave.

"Uh, Amie," I hear a moment later. My heart jumps.

"What?"

"This is weird," Jane says, "but I think I just lost the mucus plug."

In that moment, I forge an irreversible synaptic link between *Blue Crush* and "mucus plug," and, in the same moment, become convinced that Jane's coworker is a witch. Whatever we stimulated seems to have awoken. Jane is opening up, beginning to move. We are getting closer. But then nothing else happens. Her contractions continue to come and go, starting and stopping, flirting with birth.

We wait, and watch the surfer girl swim back out to sea.

Two days later, in the wee hours of the morning, Jane shakes me awake. I look at the clock on the dresser. It is 1:48 a.m. She is having contractions, she tells me. We pull on our robes and go into the living room. I remember that the childbirth educators encouraged Husbands-and-Partners to make toast or other bland food for the mom-to-be in the early stages of labor. I toast half a bagel and give it to Jane, who has moved to the living-room sofa. I sit in the chair across from her, gripping a watch to time her contractions and a notepad to track them.

"Tell me when the next one starts," I say repeatedly. She has a few more and then the contractions taper off. We climb back into bed with the cats, whose looming suspicion is making them simultaneously cloying and wary. One perches on Jane's hip, and the other presses himself against her arm.

I have hoped all along that the baby might be born on March 19, our anniversary. Now it looks as though it might actually happen. Jane has all the classic signs of early labor: bloody show, cramping, lots of mucus, contractions that hang around for a while and then disappear, fatigue, lower back pain. We are there, on the cusp.

But in the morning, there are no signs of contractions, other than the same general tightness that Jane has felt for days. I rub her Achilles tendons some more. I make carbohydrate-heavy meals so that Jane will be prepared and ready for the big race, whenever it starts. But so far, she is still warming up, stretching out, literally getting limber. She is working on her Mental Game, envisioning labor as a long and uphill cross-country ski, a one-woman Birkebeiner. She is mapping out hills in her mind, hills that get bigger and closer together, uphill and downhill, going and coming.

In the afternoon, we go for a walk by Lake of the Isles in Minneapolis, a lake that can't quite decide if it is really a swamp. Its muddy waters overflow regularly in spring and summer, but even so, it attracts a quiet following of readers and picnickers eating gourmet takeout from plastic containers. Today, it is as soft and still as usual, the remains of winter clinging in patches to the shore.

We circled this lake almost daily in our old, pre-pregnant life. Today, we move slowly, cautiously. Jane lumbers like a large and unwieldy animal, while I watch vigilantly for any lingering ice. Glancing up, I see an unusually large bird gliding toward us. I am a fan of birds of prey, so long as they remain at the safe distance of twenty feet or more, and I want to see if I can identify this one. It doesn't fly like a crow, and it doesn't have the arced wings of a hawk. It drops altitude and floats low and languidly over our heads. It's a bald eagle. There are eagles in the area, but we have never seen one anywhere near this lake. I feel as though we have received a blessing. We stand and watch the eagle, Jane bursting with baby, my hand on her back.

"It's going to be OK," Jane says. "I'm ready."

FIVE

Shock and Awe

[1]   3/19

AT JUST PAST 3:00 A.M., I look through a glass window into the operating room where Jane lies on a table being sewn back together. All I see is white and red: the white lights and walls of the surgical room; the red of Jane's blood. A screaming baby, apparently mine, lies in front of me on a warm white table under a lamp. A doctor, an older man with white hair and glasses, is rubbing her dry. Her hands and feet are still slightly blue. Thick dark hair creeps down her forehead and rings her face, giving her tiny sideburns. Creamy vernix, colored yellow by the meconium swimming in the amniotic fluid, clings to her crevices and fills the crannies of her ears. She looks like she has been rubbed in butter.

The doctor pushes a suction tube, thin as a coffee stirrer, into her nose and pulls it back out, checking for any inhaled fluid. He seems satisfied.

I am wearing a face mask, surgical cap, and oversized paper booties, as instructed by a nurse earlier in the evening. I stare at the baby on the table. Her arms are flung open. Her legs kick. She bellows.

"Good lungs," the doctor says with an approving nod.

Nurses lob Apgar numbers in my direction. I no longer remember what any of them mean, but everyone here seems pleased.

Time has stopped momentarily. I am only vaguely aware of the movement of the nurses. My attention is wholly fixated on the child in front of me. I hang in a sort of limbo, suspended between one life and another: my past and my future, my life and hers. I barely know what to do. I barely remember how to breathe. This baby is a stranger to me and she is my intimate, all at once.

"You can touch her," the doctor nudges. I realize that I haven't done so yet. I inhale and hold my breath. I reach a hand slowly toward her. I stroke her gently, gingerly, gliding my fingers across her stomach and her chest. She is soft, still moist, a little sticky. Here, in front of me, is idea made flesh. I am touching my daughter. I am touching the soft, slippery skin of hope.

I knew that birth would be painful, but I thought it would be exhilarating, an opening into the world, a letting go. Instead, it was fear. It was prayer. It was a cold, shivering shudder.

I thought I had a pretty good idea of what to expect. I imagined that Jane would go into labor at home, that she would have increasingly intense pain, and that she would sit on our bouncy green exercise ball under the pulsing water of the shower just like Paula did in the video we watched in our childbirth education class. I imagined that I would make her dry toast and warm tea. I would rub her back and she would cry out when the contractions peaked.

I imagined that, once we got to the hospital, I would walk the hallways of the maternity ward with Jane, stopping when she needed to rest, her hand on my shoulder. I would play the music Jane had carefully selected weeks before, and she would hold on to me and sway. We hired a doula, a woman trained to provide emotional and physical support to laboring women. I imagined that she would be with us in the labor room, laying socks filled with warm, dry rice on Jane's back and neck to relax her, rubbing her arms and legs to release tension. I would feed Jane ice chips just like supportive partners are apparently supposed to do. I would cheer her on.

I imagined that Jane would get to the pushing stage of labor and that she would heave against the stacked pillows on the bed, her legs held back to allow the baby the widest possible opening. I would begin to see the baby's head, wet with blood and water, peeking out of Jane. I would tell her, "I can see the baby. She's almost here." I would see the baby crown, see her head emerge into the world, see her slip and crawl out of Jane's body. I imagined that I would watch the doctor catch her in his hands, red and wet. I imagined that I would hear our baby's first scream, that Jane would begin to cry, that the doctor would put the baby on Jane's chest, that this would be the way our daughter came into the world.

In some ways, this is more real to me than what happened.

Jane's contractions begin late in the afternoon on Tuesday, March 18. We have been expecting them for days, lying in wait. Unlike the contractions of the previous few days, these don't tease. They hold steady, coming every twenty minutes or so. We have been told again and again that this stage of labor usually takes, oh, a very long time and that we should not rush to the hospital. So, as the childbirth instructors recommended, we decide to have a bland dinner (scrambled eggs and toast) and then go to a movie. We drive to a theater to see *Chicago*. I bring a pen and a memo pad so that I can track Jane's contractions. Despite all our planning, we have arrived at labor without a watch that has a second hand, so we stop at Target and buy a digital watch that lights up in fluorescent green. When the movie starts, Jane squeezes my leg at the start of each spasm and releases her grip at its end. I scribble the times of each stop and start in my notebook. Even without the watch, it is clear that Jane's squeezing is becoming noticeably more frequent. By the end of the movie, her contractions last sixty to ninety seconds and come every five minutes. We don't stay for the credits.

At home, I change into the clothes I have selected for the birth (old jeans, sports bra, long-sleeved t-shirt) and put our hospital bags in the car. I lay a beach towel on the passenger seat, as we have been advised to do in case Jane's water breaks on the way to the hospital. I spill extra food into the cats' bowls.

A little after ten o'clock, Jane calls Cindy, the doula whom we hired a couple of months ago. She has promised to see us through this birth. Cindy brings experience, reassurance, calm—all the things that I am lacking. I am ecstatic to pay her $250 fee; in truth, I would pay far more. We met with Cindy at a coffee shop about a month ago to discuss Jane's birth plan. Jane has spoken with her a few times over the past couple of weeks to update her on the early signs and symptoms of impending birth.

"I think it's happening," Jane says into the phone. Cindy asks if she can still talk through the contractions. "Some of them," Jane replies. Cindy reminds her that this could continue for quite a while, especially with a first birth. She suggests that we report back after an hour or so.

In the living room, Jane sits on the rubber exercise ball that I brought up from the basement. She has one hand on her belly and clutches my arm with her other hand. I sit on the sofa next to her and rub her back as she moves slowly back and forth on the ball. At each contraction, she drops her head down, her chin folding into her neck. She is nearly silent, breathing in, breathing out.

Meanwhile, I monitor the time. The contractions become more frequent. Within half an hour, they're coming every three to four minutes. This time, I call Cindy. She agrees that we should go to the hospital and asks me to call her after Jane is admitted. "Remember, they might not think she's ready to be admitted yet. It all depends on how far along she is," she says.

We pile ourselves into the car. Jane grips the armrest. I tuck the directions to the hospital into the change holder next to the front seat, lest I lose my mind and forget the way. At just past eleven o'clock, we pull out of the driveway and into the dark night.

I drive through the normally congested streets, thanking God that Jane managed to avoid going into labor at rush hour. Jane is quiet, her breathing becoming more intentional and less involuntary with each contraction. I still stop at red lights.

I realize, upon arriving at the hospital, that I never found out which entrance to use. We always went to the education building for our childbirth classes. I know that the maternity ward is on the sixth floor of the hospital, but I don't know how to get there. So I pick a door. Jane sits in the car while I go inside to find out if this is the right way in. A security guard asks me what I need.

"Maternity," I say. He clearly doesn't want a baby born at his post, so he grabs a wheelchair and asks where the patient is. He pushes the chair out to the car, loads Jane in, and begins to push her swiftly toward the birthing center. I trot alongside. He gets us to the maternity ward and, looking profoundly relieved, leaves us there.

A group of nurses are sitting in the Maternal Assessment Center. Jane rests her head on the reception desk counter.

"What are you here for?" a nurse asks.

"Birth," Jane groans.

The nurses nod knowingly at each other. "Full moon," one of them says. "Busy night."

One of the nurses comes to the desk and begins to pull together the admissions paperwork. She cannot find Jane's file, despite the fact that we preregistered months ago, so she begins a new file. I go back outside to move the car and get our supplies, now packed and repacked several times over. Eventually, I return with our bag of clothes, a pillow, a CD player, and several CDs.

A different nurse leads Jane and me into an assessment room. She instructs Jane to lie down on the table and pull up her shirt. She attaches a fetal monitor to Jane's belly. Its two flat metal disks, like microphones secured with a wide elastic belt, tune in to the baby's sounds and movements. I stand by the side of the bed in the narrow room, our belongings wedged into a corner, and we watch Hannah's heartbeat register on the monitor, consistently running between 137 and 145. Strong and true.

"I want to see how far you've dilated," the nurse says. She slides Jane's sweatpants down and reaches her gloved hand between Jane's legs. "You're just at one centimeter." Jane has been at one centimeter since last Friday. "You might need to go home for a while until you progress further," she adds.

"But she's having contractions every two to three minutes," I say. When do they want her back? Every thirty seconds? We're not going anywhere. They can send us away, but we will not leave the lobby.

"I'll come back in about twenty minutes to check the strip," the nurse says, pointing to the monitor. "Then we can see how you're doing."

Jane has another contraction and the beeps on the monitor begin to slow. I stick my head out the door and flag the nurse. The microphone apparently slipped out of place during the contraction, so the nurse adjusts it and belts it back into place.

Jane lies on her side on the table, hooked to the beeping machine. I hold a glass of ice water for her to sip while Hannah continues to tick away. Jane says nothing, just clenches my hand during contractions. I watch the monitor behind Jane's head, the lines spiking with each contraction, the heartbeat steady and strong.

The nurse comes back to check the monitor and frowns at the printout. "I'm having trouble getting a reactive strip," she says. "Let's leave you on a while longer."

"What's a reactive strip?" I ask.

"We want to see the baby's heartbeat accelerate during contractions," she explains. "Usually we like to see that happen three times in a twenty-minute period. It's a sign of fetal well-being."

Does this mean that the baby is in distress? Apparently, Hannah's steadiness is not what we want. I continue to watch the monitor. 138. 147. 142. 145. 142.

After another fifteen minutes, the nurse returns. "We're going to have you roll onto your other side," she says. "Sometimes positioning the baby a little differently gives us the response we're looking for." Jane maneuvers gingerly onto her left side, the nurse holding the wires that attach to the monitor that judges our baby's state of well-being.

The nurse remains in the room, monitoring the monitor. Jane squeezes my hand and moans. The number on the monitor begins to drop. 140. 132. 128. The nurse moves the microphone, explaining that the baby may have turned away. She moves the two disks in circles on Jane's belly. 122. 116. The nurse steps outside the room and calls another nurse in. They move the microphones around some more. The heartbeat continues to fall.

"She's slowing down," the nurse says. "We need to go." 102. 93. 88. 82. The nurses quickly detach the microphones and open a double door into a hallway.

"Where are you going?" I ask.

"To surgery," one of them says. "We have to get the baby out."

I try to walk through the door with Jane as they wheel her bed through, but there is not enough room. I step back. Jane looks up. "Stay with me," she says. And then she's gone.

It feels like a dream, even in the moment. I see myself walking through the hospital hallway, following Jane, whose gurney speeds ahead. People in green and burgundy scrubs appear from various directions, rushing to the operating room. A hurried nurse points to a closet where, she says, I can find scrubs. I pull them over my clothes and cover my shoes with the plastic booties. I pull what looks like a shower cap over my hair and position a mask over my nose and mouth. I barely know what I am doing. I go back into the hallway, where a couple of nurses are sitting at a desk. Jane is gone. The rushing is over.

"I'm here with Jane Miller," I say to one of the nurses. "What's going on?"

"They're getting her prepped for surgery," she says. "You can have a seat over there." I don't move. "That's our official waiting seat," the nurse prompts. "They'll call you when they're ready." I sit down.

I try not to cry. I try to pray. I hardly ever pray, so it's very simple: Let Jane be all right. Let Hannah be all right. I wait.

A nurse appears and tells me that the baby's heart rate has stabilized. Our doctor has been called and is on his way. When he arrives, he will assess the situation.

She leads me into the operating room. I am surprised at how barren it is: stark white walls, bright lights, an operating table in the middle of the room. Electrical cords are everywhere. There is a straight-back wooden chair next to the operating table. Jane lies on her side on the table. Nurses and technicians stand on point. I sit in the chair and hold Jane's hand.

"They're waiting for the doctor," she says. "I think the nurse panicked." It is 1:15 a.m. I watch the clock. We wait.

Jane's water has broken and it's clear, from its green hue, that there is meconium in it. The nurses have now hooked Jane up to a urinary catheter, so there is one more line attached to her body.

About ten minutes later, our doctor appears, scrubbed and ready to operate. He studies the fetal monitor chart.

"I don't think that we need to do surgery right now," he says to Jane. "It doesn't mean that it won't happen later. But the baby's heart rate has stabilized. It could have been a fluke. I think we should wait and see what happens."

The doctor recommends putting an internal fetal monitor on the baby, however, to keep an eye on what's going on inside. I sit in my chair and watch as he removes the monitor, which looks something like a twelve-inch antenna, from its sterile wrapper and manipulates it inside Jane, attaching it to the baby's scalp. Jane squeezes my hand. I run my hand across her hair.

It's clear by now that any residual ideas of natural childbirth that we might be harboring are shot. Jane is restricted to lying on her side or her back, hooked inside and out to monitors and catheters and bags. The doctor asks Jane if she wants an epidural. She answers immediately. Yes. Please. Now would be good. The anesthetist has already left the operating room, but the doctor says that he will call her back.

The nurses pack up Jane and her tubes and wheel her gurney to a labor room. I follow, padding through the hospital hallway in my green booties. In the labor room, I stand again by the side of the bed. I am vaguely aware of the nurses checking equipment, watching monitors, reading printouts. Somewhere in the background, the clock ticks toward 2:00 a.m. Jane lies on her side on the bed. She barely moves. She is wholly focused, like a Tibetan monk, entirely attentive to the forces that hold her in their grip and entirely disconnected from anything that does not serve those forces. With each contraction, she shuts her eyes and exhales through rounded lips. She moans, but only quietly, her voice sounding as though it is coming through thick and distant fog. I have forgotten all the helpful techniques we learned in childbirth class. The only thing I can think to do is hold her hand, pet her hair, and tell her that she's doing a great job and that I'm here with her.

And then, thank you God, our doula walks through the door. When we didn't call her back to say that Jane had been admitted to the hospital (which, to be precise, she still has not), Cindy called to check. She was told that the patient was in the operating room. She got into her car and began to drive.

Cindy immediately leans in close to Jane and helps her adjust her breathing so that she can relax during the short intervals between contractions. She strokes Jane's arm, as though she is brushing the pain out through Jane's fingertips.

Jane opens her eyes. "Where's the epidural?" she asks. Twenty minutes have gone by. A nurse tells us that the anesthetist is on her way but got sidelined by a Code Blue. She asks Jane to rate her level of pain on a scale of one to ten, with ten being the most pain she can imagine. "About a nine," Jane says and closes her eyes.

The heart monitor beeps like water dripping from a leaky faucet.

At about 2:45, the anesthetist arrives. After the Code Blue, she had been called for two other patients. We have finally made it to the top of the list. It has taken forty minutes.

As the anesthetist sets up her supplies, a nurse comes to check how far Jane has dilated. She inserts her gloved hand beneath the sheet, stares fixedly into the air, and reports that Jane is at five centimeters. It took Jane over a week to get to one centimeter; now she has reached five in just a couple of hours.

The anesthetist explains that she will insert the epidural into Jane's spinal column and that Jane should begin to feel relief "soon." The anesthetist begins the litany, like a recital of Miranda, of the possible repercussions of having an epidural. Among them: back pain, spinal headache, nausea, death. Has any woman, in this situation, ever reconsidered? Jane indicates that she understands and accepts the risks.

"OK, then. We'll have you sit up and lean over as far as you can, as though you are encircling the baby. That will help open up the space where we'll insert the catheter."

A cadre of nurses appears and begins rearranging the cords snaking from Jane's body. Jane sits up and puts her feet over the side of the bed. She leans forward. I stand to her left and Cindy to her right. Jane cradles her head in the space formed by our shoulders.

"I'm going to insert a test dose first," the anesthetist says. "Then we'll be able to set the level for the drip."

The anesthetist presses her fingers on Jane's spine, finding the right spot. She rubs antiseptic in a circle with a cotton pad and then inserts the needle. It goes in without complication. Jane is now hooked to another tube and bag, this one hanging on a portable IV stand. The nurses ease Jane back onto the bed, rearranging her coils of cords.

Cindy leans over Jane and tells her to let her breath all out, to release fully as a contraction ends. I hear Cindy's voice, a soothing, drawling counterpoint to Jane's low moaning. I hear the heart monitor, beeping like a metronome.

And then it begins to slow.

What I hear are the silences. Jane becomes tense and attentive, listening. I see nurses moving around the room, although I am not aware of any sound they are making. I watch a nurse who stands on the other side of Jane's bed, staring at the numbers on the monitor. Behind Jane's head, I can see the numbers, lit blood red.

145.

125.

111.

100.

I feel myself beginning to panic. The nurse waits and watches.

95.

87.

"What's happening?" Jane whispers. "What's happening to Hannah?"

74.

65.

Everything is still except for this dreadful disappearing sound. We are in suspended animation. I barely breathe.

56.

50.

I see people moving around. I don't know what they are doing. The nurse still stares at the monitor, unmoving.

45.

"Let's go," someone says sharply. People spring into motion. The nurse who had been watching the monitor yanks the IV bag off its pole and puts it on Jane's bed next to her catheter bag. Another nurse releases the brakes on her gurney and begins pulling the bed toward the door. I watch as Jane is rushed out the door.

A moment later, I am back in the chair opposite the nurses' desk. This time, Cindy sits in a chair next to me. She is telling me what will happen in the operating room.

"They'll probably give her general anesthesia," Cindy says, "because there wasn't enough time for the epidural to take effect." She says something else. I don't hear it.

A fear that has been biting at my heart rises sickeningly to the surface. I will not be allowed to keep both Jane and Hannah. The fates are demanding a trade. I don't want this. It's a price I cannot pay.

Time ticks. A minute. Two. Three.

A woman dressed in surgical scrubs appears in the hallway. She must be here to take me into the operating room, I think. They must be ready to start.

"Do you want to come see her?" she asks. "She's screaming for you."

I get up out of the chair and follow her blindly. Only then do I realize that it is Hannah who is calling. She is here. She is born.

3/20

We do almost nothing but hold her.

Hannah is delicious. Her dark hair—brown, nearly black—lies soft and silken on her head, like a cap swirling from her crown. Her eyes squint open and then snap shut again, not yet ready to take in too much of the world. Her lips are finely shaped, pursing and then rounding into an O, as if she is surprised to be here. She wants to suck, working her lips in feeding motions before, during and after meals. Her ears are soft and floppy. Her belly rises in a soft mound. I can wrap my thumb and forefinger around her thigh. Her fingers are wrinkled and creased, like artifacts on this new body. We take turns holding her, lying side by side in the hospital room, Jane on the adjustable bed and I on the foldout cot next to her.

We never really learn what went wrong during the birth. When the doctor comes to check on Jane and Hannah, he tells us that Hannah had an unusually short umbilical cord. We also learn that somehow, during labor, she had shifted from a head-down position to a sideways position. Was the umbilical cord being squeezed, reducing her blood and oxygen supply? We don't know.

Sometimes, when Jane is not resting or we are not staring dumbfoundedly at Hannah, we turn on the television. I sit on the cot, holding Hannah, who is asleep in my arms. For months, Jane has congratulated herself for orchestrating a pregnancy in which she would be due to deliver during March Madness. She loves the endless rounds of college basketball and planned to introduce Hannah to her hoops-obsessed Hoosier heritage immediately after birth.

Instead, we have war. Hannah was born and U.S. forces attacked Iraq virtually simultaneously. Every channel this morning is war, every reporter talking about war. On the television screen, we watch a journalist report on the attack while bombs explode like a laser show in the background. I hold Hannah close to my chest and watch the flashing lights on the screen. I touch her butter-soft skin. I listen to her breathing. I pat her bottom. Meanwhile, the reporter talks about troop advancements and the promise of our military to deliver a "shock and awe" campaign. What are we getting into? I don't know if we have brought Hannah into a world that is falling apart. I don't know if her future will be defined by whatever this war is. Right now, all I really know is that she is here, in my arms.

Sometime in the early evening, I pad across the hospital hallway in my socks. There is a kitchenette across from our room, stocked with tea and orange juice and cereal and bread for toast. I make a cup of tea for Jane and one for myself. We have spent the last hour and a half patting Hannah, who has all the signs of gas, or so we are told. We rolled her feet toward her torso and massaged her tummy. Maybe it helped. She stopped crying, at least, and began nursing again. Jane lies propped up in the hospital bed working on getting a proper latch. We are alone with Hannah temporarily: no nurses or doctors or lactation consultants, no visitors or phone calls. Jane has turned the television off. It is quiet.

An older man who looks like he must be a new grandfather comes over to the kitchenette while I am heating water. He inspects the dregs of coffee still standing in the pot, then gives me a tired smile and walks away. At the end of the hallway, a couple is just arriving at the Maternal Assessment Center. She is roundly pregnant. He is carrying a duffel bag and a CD player, just like the one we brought and never touched. They look anxious.

I watch them and feel like I have crossed over. I wish them well, wish them a smooth crossing. I hope birth goes the way they want it to. I hope they get some use out of their CD player. I hope they have a beautiful baby. I hope for peace.

3/21

I have returned home to get some clean clothes because the C-section means that our stay in the hospital will be twice as long as we had anticipated. I give the cats some extra food and water, stack the mail on the dining-room table, and grab a couple of *New Yorkers* for Jane and a book for me. My father and stepmother have sent an enormous bouquet of flowers, which stands shivering outside our front door. Our house feels familiar, but foreign, like a country where I lived once but long since left. I feel an urgency to return to the hospital, which suddenly is more familiar than our home.

I don't know who I am right now, nor where I live. I am in transit between two worlds. I am a mother, but I barely know what that means. I hold my child, but I barely know her. Mostly, I feel stunned. I stand at the border of a new world, but I am still outside, peering through the keyhole.

I load the clothes and books into the car and pull out of the driveway. I turn on the radio. Normally, I listen to public radio, but it is nonstop talk about the war in Iraq and I just cannot listen to any more of it right now. I find a station that is playing music from the early 1980s. Someone is singing, as usual, about falling hopelessly in love.

I am half-listening to the music. I am exhausted and overwhelmed and, without realizing it, I have started to cry. I wipe my eyes on my shirtsleeve. And there, I smell Hannah. Her baby scent clings to me. Somewhere between changing a diaper and swaddling her in a flannel blanket and attempting to burp her and trying to soothe her while she wails, Hannah has rubbed off on me. I hold my sleeve against my face and breathe in her scent. I need to return to her. I need to hold her close to me. My tears magnify her smell. I am still working on absorbing the reality that Hannah is my daughter and I am her mother, but I have begun to fall in love.

3/22

On the fourth day, we bring Hannah home. I think this is completely insane. I want to stay at the hospital. I feel safe there. We have all that I can imagine needing: a private room, a bathroom, and a cafeteria where I can buy ice cream sandwiches. Admittedly, the food they serve to Jane is questionable, but I can supplement it with food from the cafeteria and bowls of cereal from the kitchenette across the hall. What matters is that there are trained nurses just down the corridor. If something goes terribly wrong, we can get immediate help. Hannah is still jaundiced, I think. We are so clueless that we thought she had a lovely golden skin tone. Isn't this proof that we need to stay? Jane is having trouble with nursing. Shouldn't we stay until that gets worked out? I'm scared to death to be at home with the baby. Isn't that reason enough to stay?

But the hospital and the insurance company are kicking us out. Against all evidence to the contrary, they say we're ready. It's time to go.

In the morning, I make a trip back to the house to transport the many bouquets of flowers we have received from friends and family and coworkers, leaving a couple behind on the maternity ward for the nurses. I take our luggage into the empty house. I give the cats one of Hannah's baby blankets, hoping that they will grow accustomed to her scent and resigned to her presence in the couple of hours before we bring her through the door. The cats sniff the blanket, but seem profoundly uninterested, clinging to the belief that their humans have just been off on a self-indulgent vacation and will return home shortly to life as normal.

I drive back to the hospital to get Jane and Hannah and bring them home. Jane is sitting on the hospital bed, Hannah sucking away at her breast.

"Are you ready?" I ask.

"As I'll ever be," she says.

I carefully dress Hannah in the outfit I selected before her birth. It is ridiculously large on her, but it's so pretty, with its tiny rosebud print, that I ignore the bagginess. Jane pulls on her coat and slides her still-swollen feet into shoes that she has loosened as much as possible.

The nurse comes to the room with a wheelchair for Jane. Jane holds Hannah until we get downstairs, while I carry the empty car seat. The hospital won't let us leave without a properly installed car seat, not that I would ever dream of doing so. In fact, a month or so before Hannah was born, I took our car to the local police station to have a Trained Officer check to see whether my attempt at installing the car seat was adequate. It was most definitely not. Trained Officer Dave gave me a talk about the importance of seat belts, car seats, and defensive driving, and then made himself into a human shoehorn in the back seat of the car, jamming the car seat into place.

Now, the car seat is the only thing that is secure. I buckle Hannah into the carrier and snap it, as though I know what I'm doing, into the base of the seat. Jane eases herself from wheelchair to passenger seat, the nurse reminding her that she cannot drive for two weeks or lift anything heavier than ten pounds for six weeks. I take a deep breath and get behind the wheel.

This will make me find religion.

I put the car in drive and pull out at a steady ten miles per hour. It might take us two hours to get home, but I intend to be safe. I don't even consider taking the highway, which scares me on the best of days. I stay on the side streets, trying to avoid the potholes that spatter the roads. I slow down when I think the street lights may be ready to turn yellow. We crawl home.

Finally, we arrive. Jane unfolds herself from the car and I carry the baby, who, in her car seat, is too heavy for Jane to lift. We venture inside. I feel a need to introduce Hannah to the house, perhaps to give her a tour. "This is where you live now, Hannah," I say. Later I'll tell her about how we tore up the forty-year-old wool carpets and refinished the hardwood floors after we bought the place, and how the pink-tiled bathroom reminds her grandpa of the one in his childhood home in Iowa.

Jane sits gingerly on the sofa and arranges a couple of pillows by her sides. I lay Hannah on her lap. Louise, our calico cat, immediately climbs onto Jane's lap and curls up next to Hannah. Jane is delighted, even though the other cat is cowering somewhere in the basement.

I sit down. I risk a breath.

Suddenly it occurs to me.

"Where is she going to sleep?" I ask.

Of course, we have a crib, which has been standing empty in the nursery for months. But now I cannot imagine actually putting Hannah into it, which would mean putting her into her room. Which would mean that she would be separate from us. While we were in the hospital, we took Hannah to the nursery at night so that Jane and I could get some sleep while people who actually knew what they were doing watched over her. That was fine; a relief, even. But the prospect of leaving Hannah all alone in a separate room—while we sleep, no less—is unthinkable.

Not long ago, I couldn't imagine having her in bed with us. We know about the philosophy of the family bed, of course, and how much more natural some people say it is to have parents and kids all cuddled up together like a little pile of kittens. Then I read a book advocating the family bed that noted that children usually wean themselves of it around four or five. *Years.* This is not happening in our home, I decided. We bought a crib for a reason. But now that Hannah is actually here, putting her in the crib seems appalling, like sending her into dangerous and cruel exile.

I have spent the past several months making sure that everything is ready for this moment, and now I find myself on a hurried trip to the store. I go to the closest baby supply store and buy a bassinette. They have only limited choices, so I am stuck with a ridiculously ugly fiberboard and foam structure decorated with pictures of smiling cherubs in yellow and sea foam green.

When I get home, I snap it together, a bit of the cheap lacy edge tearing in the process. I set it up next to our bed. When Hannah falls asleep, I take her from Jane's arms and set her in the bassinette. She wakes. She cries. She reacts like Goldilocks: oh, no, this bed is much too hard. Or perhaps it's much too ugly. So Jane and I take turns holding her, cuddled to our chests, while one by one, we doze, propped against pillows.

Day becomes night becomes day. We make it.

3/23

I dream that Jane goes for a walk around a lake and her incision tears open and begins to bleed uncontrollably.

I dream that Jane and I are in the basement with Hannah and a foot-long brown rat scurries out from a corner.

I dream that Hannah stops breathing.

I dream that I can't breathe.

3/24

I am captivated. I am enchanted. I am spellbound.

3/25

We have been thrust into a parallel universe where planning and time are irrelevant. I have always been devoted to planning: short-term, long-term, I like it all. In high school, I planned my day down to the quarter hour.

None of it matters now. I can make plans, but I cannot implement them. Day and night move in three-hour increments that cycle in endless succession. Our goals have been reduced to the lowest common denominator: run a load of laundry, get Hannah to eat more, try to sleep. I transfer my need to plan into an obsession with charting. On scraps of paper, I track Hannah's feedings and soilings. Food in, food out. Our lives are defined by the most primitive workings of the human body: learning to eat, learning to breathe, learning to sleep.

Meanwhile, I am losing my sense of judgment. When I go out to run an errand, I sit in my car at the intersection, stymied by the question of whether or not to turn.

I, who love control, have apparently lost it. If the baby is wailing, she is wailing. If she is awake, she is awake. What I do seems to have little bearing on what actually happens. Cause and effect are separating, held together only by tenuous threads of hope.

I have also lost my sense of time. I struggle to remember what day it is. Truthfully, I no longer care. Does it matter if it's Monday or Wednesday? All that matters now is this moment: Is the baby crying? Is she sleeping? Is she hungry? Is she happy?

In the space of just a few nights, I have slipped from the functional adult world to the newborn netherworld. During the day, I feel like I am moving through thick air, as though the atmosphere has gelled into pudding. At night, I yearn to sleep but yet am unwilling to do so. Instead, I doze, listening constantly for cries, for whimpers, for the gasping, gurgling sounds of newborn lungs. I have become less aware of what is happening around me and more aware of what is happening, or might be happening, or could happen, to this child. In pregnancy, the body compensates for deficits of required vitamins or minerals by mining what is needed to build the baby from the body of the mother. After birth, apparently, the parental brain continues to preference the baby, directing all mental function to the protection of the child. We live in a three-person cocoon, bound together by silky threads. Our normal lives have become not only meaningless, but a distraction. All I want is to hold Hannah. All I want is to feel her breath, soft as a moth's wings, on my cheek.

[11]

I am obsessed with excrement. I call the nurse, even though it is Sunday, to ask how concerned I should be if we have not had a soiled diaper in thirty-six hours. Wets, yes. Stools, no. Now two-and-a-half weeks old, Hannah has been a slow starter in this arena. The nurse is reassuring, suggesting that Hannah might just be a "reluctant pooper." She advises me to give the baby a sitz bath, to kind of warm things up down there. If that doesn't work, she says, try a little anal sphincter stimulation with a rectal thermometer. If that doesn't work, try half of a glycerin suppository. If that doesn't work, good Lord.

And so we begin. Jane pours a bowl of warm water and we dip our baby's little bottom in it. She screeches and urinates. Nothing else.

We put a little KY jelly on the rectal thermometer and give the anal stimulation a go. I cannot believe we are doing this. We are lesbians, for God's sake. The only lesbians I have ever known who thought about anal stimulation were the women who always scared me when we lived in New York.

Still no stool, so we decide to give up for a while. Jane carries Hannah into the living room where she slumps down into the over-sized blue armchair, the baby lying in her arms. Hannah is feeling mellow, now that we are not dipping her in bowls of water and coming at her with gooey probes. She begins to root around Jane's chest where she knows hidden food awaits. Her mouth hangs open, like a baby robin groping for a worm. Jane pulls her shirt up with a look of resignation. The fatigue of new parenthood is setting in like a slow, looming storm front. The adrenaline of the early days has dripped away. Hannah sucks for ten minutes or so and then falls blissfully into sleep.

Jane sets Hannah—gently, gently—into her carrier and tucks a pink-checked flannel blanket around her legs. We go into the kitchen to make lunch.

"Why did we do this?" Jane asks.

"It seemed like a good idea at the time," I mutter.

It's surprising how quickly you wear down. The worry of new parenthood is far worse than I anticipated. The anxiety is intense. Hannah rasps and gurgles in the night and I leap up to make sure she is still breathing. Her umbilical cord is seeping a little: Does that mean something is wrong? She spits up and I have no way of knowing what is normal and what is too much. If she soaks half of her bib, is that too much? Are three spit-ups okay, but six too many? Is this gastroesophageal reflux? Or is it just infancy?

I dread the evening because I know that the anxiety always gets worse after dark. With dusk comes fear. I tell myself that I needn't be so worried. We have a support network, Hannah has checked out well at all her doctor's visits, and we have access to a twenty-four-hour nurse line. But at night, worries become obsessive and remote possibilities become impending certainties. I wait each night for the dawn.

Jane and I feast on each other's anxieties. One of us worries about something, anything, whether reasonable or not (but best if it contains a kernel of possibility, a morsel of fact), and plants the seed in the other's mind. Finding fertile soil, it takes root. It grows. We offer halfhearted reassurances: "I was just reading about encopresis, which is really terrible, but it usually doesn't occur until later. She probably won't develop it." Meanwhile, each of us knows that the fear is growing, that the assurances are not heartfelt. And just as we know this, we know that we are feeding our own neuroses. And just as we know *that*, we become less and less able to do anything about it. We each withdraw, pulling back behind our own veil of worry.

"I think she's fine," I say. "But of course, we can call the doctor. Do you want to?" (You're It.)

"No. I don't think we need to call. What's she doing? Is she all right?" (Now you.)

"She's okay. I just wish she would have a stool. I can't believe it's been thirty-six hours." (Your turn.)

"Why's she crying again? Should we call the doctor?" (Back to you.)

"I don't know. Maybe. What do you think?"

And on it goes.

My cousin, mother of two miraculously grown children, calls to check in. I tell her the Saga of the Stool. Stephanie suggests that we bicycle Hannah's legs (already doing that), hold her vertically (gravity), and try not to worry (hopeless). As we are talking, Hannah begins to screech. Jane waves at me and says that she thinks it's time for the suppository. I get off the phone. Jane carries Hannah into the nursery and puts her on the changing table. The glycerin suppositories, made for children, look impossibly enormous, like waxy ballistic missiles. I take one from the bottle and cut it down by two-thirds, attempting to mold the edges to something that looks a little softer, a little less invasive. We are ready.

Jane removes the diaper and almost whoops. There is a poo. Not a huge one, but not a smudge. We are thrilled. I put the suppository back into the bottle, we clean Hannah up, and we go back into the living room, grinning giddily. I am so pleased that I call Stephanie to report.

"The eagle has landed," I say.

She's as excited as I am. This must be the bond that holds parents together: shared excitement over basic bodily functions that are otherwise not discussed in polite company.

"That's wonderful," she says, and I know she means it. "Things are moving."

We sink into the sofa, Jane cradling Hannah. I am exhausted. I feel like I'm in boot camp, but at least we have had a victory. We have made it another day.

A week later, we become convinced that Hannah has cystic fibrosis. The beauty of this anxiety is that it has some degree of rational basis because Jane carries the most common genetic mutation that causes the disease. Although we confirmed long ago that our sperm bank screens all its donors for the most common mutations and does not accept anyone who tests positive, we still worry.

I scrutinize the entry on cystic fibrosis in the *Boston Children's Hospital Guide to Your Child's Health and Development*—which we own—and learn that symptoms include wheezing, coughing, and digestive problems. Every time Hannah wheezes, snorts, grunts, gasps, or spits up, all of which she does with regularity, I am convinced that it is confirmation of chronic illness.

We learn that the initial test for cystic fibrosis is a sweat test. The doctor collects a little sweat from the child and measures the saline content. An elevated salt level can signal a positive result. I stay up at night and feel my heart clench when Hannah snorts. Jane admits that she has secretly been licking the back of Hannah's neck to taste for salt.

By the time Hannah is ten weeks old, we have mostly let go of our cystic fibrosis worries. Now we think she might be deaf. She doesn't turn her head at our voices and she doesn't startle at loud sounds. I try to test her hearing by ringing the doorbell. No response. I snap my fingers. No response. Jane and I begin sneaking up on the poor child and clapping behind her head. No response. We remind each other that she does seem to listen to music and calm down when the bathroom fan is running. But these could be anomalies. Clap. Nothing. I begin searching the Internet for resources on hearing impairments. I should know better by now. I quickly find the suggestion that parents try to test their child's hearing by clapping behind their heads.

We remind ourselves that she *had a hearing test* in the hospital and passed it just fine. But the tech was busy that day, I think. What if they just did a social promotion? Jane calls the pediatric clinic. A doctor calls back and says that the hospital test is 99 percent accurate, but there is some concern that she isn't startling.

I scurry back onto the Internet. Jane and I make a pact to stop trying to startle Hannah, at least until after her next doctor's appointment, which is in a week. I think about doing it anyway when Jane goes to the grocery store, but I resist.

Jane takes Hannah to the doctor for a checkup. Everything looks good. The doctor isn't concerned about her hearing or the startling lack of startling. She reassures Jane. Hannah gets weighed and measured, her growth noted and compared to other babies her age. At two weeks, she was below the fiftieth percentile in overall weight and now, at eleven pounds, three ounces, she is in the seventy-fifth percentile. Excellent. Her torso is exceedingly long; she has grown to twenty-four inches in total body length, putting her in the ninety-fifth percentile. But her head, which was in the ninetieth percentile for circumference, is now in the fiftieth percentile. It grew, but at a slower pace than the rest of her body.

"Do you think her head isn't growing fast enough?" Jane asks me that evening. She knows better than this. She understands statistics and the fallacy of percentiles, especially when it comes to diagnosing normality. "Do we have a pinhead baby?" I imagine Hannah all grown up: a giant torso with a head the size of a Vidalia onion. Our little Onion Head.

"I think," Jane says one day when the baby is peacefully asleep in her bouncy seat, "that I have been assuming that something is wrong with Hannah rather than expecting her to be all right."

I have also been constantly worried that there is something grave, something dreadful that has eluded the doctors, that is lurking behind the diaper pail, hiding under the crib, waiting to snatch our baby away. Some of this is a product of reading too many articles and watching too much television. We have heard the stories about sudden deaths, freak viruses, and bizarre conditions that go undetected. Some of it, also, is the product of her birth. In the moments when nurses and doctors were racing Jane toward the operating room, it seemed both to Jane and to me entirely believable, indeed likely, that something terrible—even the most terrible thing—might occur. Now, it still feels threatening to trust her to be healthy, as though we might be blindsided if we do not remain diligently on guard.

I suppose our neurosis is normal, although I sometimes wonder if it would help to have a husband in the house who would say, "Oh, for God's sake, she's fine" and turn on the Vikings game. I have made a lifelong art of worrying and I'm not about to stop now. Still, I do realize that I need to let go of at least a little of it before our pediatrician refuses to see us anymore.

It's a thin line between fear and love, a line that has become perforated since Hannah's birth. The two passions intermingle, and anxiety courses through my heart. Is it possible to love a child wholeheartedly but without fear? Or does the magnitude of our vulnerability as parents demand that we stand on guard against all dangers, real and imagined?

I lie in bed at night and watch the clock, counting the hours until dawn.

[| | |]

In mid-May, on a bright spring day, I adopt my daughter. Weirdly, the legal ties between Jane and me run most tightly through Hannah. Jane is legally her mother, and now that a judge has formally signed off on it, I am too, but Jane and I have no enforceable connection to each other beyond the paper trail we have forged through wills and powers of attorney.

Jane and I began the adoption paperwork while she was pregnant, but I could not adopt Hannah until there actually was a Hannah, an out-in-the-world Hannah, to be adopted. When we went to the hospital for the birth, I carried a manila folder containing two forms designating me as Standby Custodian—one that would allow me to make medical decisions should Jane become incapacitated before Hannah's birth and another allowing me to make decisions should something happen to Jane afterward. Since we came back from the hospital, however, I have been the legal equivalent of a live-in guest in our home.

Our lawyer, Ann, has diligently navigated us through the various required forms and procedures. She has petitioned the Minnesota Department of Human Services, requesting an Order and Decree of Adoption. She has requested a waiver of the home study, based on the facts that Jane and I have lived together since 1987 and Hannah has lived with us since she popped out into the world. Jane and I have filed an affidavit spelling out our reasons for wanting the adoption. Jane is the birth parent, it notes. Amie was present when Hannah was born. (I was in the hallway, but close enough.) The decision to have Hannah was mutual. Amie is equally involved in the care and nurture of Hannah, "including feeding, bathing, grooming, and dressing; purchasing, cleaning, and caring for her clothes; arranging for medical care, arranging for child care as needed, putting her to bed at night, attending to her during the night, waking her in the morning, and teaching elementary skills." I don't know what those elementary skills might be at this point, other than maybe lying on a blanket, but it hardly seems appropriate to quibble.

The affidavit goes on to promise, "When she is old enough to understand, we will share the nature of our relationship with her and our respective relationships to her." It points out that "Hannah needs and deserves the legal protection resulting from adoption," including not having to go through guardianship and custodianship proceedings in the event of Jane's death. The adoption will ensure my capacity to make decisions about medical care or carry Hannah on an insurance policy. It will enable Hannah to claim survivor benefits from Social Security and it protects her right to claim continuing financial support from me should I decide to become a deadbeat mom. The affidavit notes that the Court might decide that Jane's parental rights must be terminated for me to adopt Hannah, meaning that Jane would then have to adopt her as well. We file a formal request asking the Court not to require this.

We have paid the fee to search the Minnesota Fathers' Adoption Registry, as required by law, and now have a form in our possession verifying that "No putative father is registered." Ann has had her assistant take affidavits from my mother, my father, and from Jane's parents stating their support of my adoption of Hannah. Bits of personal commentary mingle with legalese in the affidavits. "We usually see Jane and Amie approximately two times per year for various social occasions." "It is very obvious watching them that they are two people who love each other." "They will show Hannah lots of love and support." Then the boilerplate: "I definitely think that it will be beneficial to Hannah to have a legal relationship with Amie as this would be a safeguard and some protection for Hannah, especially should something happen to Jane." Further Affiant sayeth not.

On the big day, we get up early and spend the entire morning getting ready. We bathe Hannah and dress her carefully in her lavender-and-white-striped pants and jacket. We break our iron out of its basement purgatory and actually press some clothes. We put on makeup. We do our hair. After two months of full-time newbornness, it feels like we are visiting a swanky and sophisticated city where we used to live.

We drive to the Hennepin County Juvenile Justice Center, where we meet Ann, as well as my sister, Stace, and our friend, Rebecca, who have come as witnesses. Ann gives us the happy news that we have been assigned to a judge she knows well. "This will be easy," she says pleasantly. In fact, there is not very much to the process, now that we have reached this point. Adoptions by same-sex partners in Hennepin County follow the protocol used for stepparent adoptions. Minnesota is not one of the ten states that officially permit second-parent adoptions by same-sex partners, but judges in some of the counties here have a track record of approving them. Hennepin County is the most reliable of all, so we feel pretty secure.

A few minutes before our appointed time, Ann reports that we have been reassigned to a new judge. "I haven't worked with him before," she says. "But he'll probably be fine." *Probably.* My feelings of security buckle. Even in mostly liberal Hennepin County, approval of second-parent adoptions is entirely contingent on the judge. The fate of my legal relationship to Hannah suddenly hangs on *probably.* Ambiguity is not what I'm looking for in this moment.

I carry Hannah into the courtroom, trying my best to look emotionally fit and bursting with maternal instinct. We stand as the judge enters the room. I try to suss out his political and religious leanings by watching him walk to the bench. He is a wiry man with curly dark hair. He confirms why we are all there. Then, God bless him, he says, "I like these kinds of cases because everyone leaves a winner."

I answer a few basic questions, mainly aimed at confirming that I understand that legal adoption means legal responsibility. Should Jane and I break up, I will still be legally responsible for Hannah's support. After running through the rote questions and admonitions, the judge approves the adoption. Then he hands out lollipops. And then we all pose for pictures, the judge, our lawyer, and Tonya, the court recorder, included.

I have carefully folded a copy of the adoption order and placed it in my wallet. I have filed four copies of Hannah's new birth certificate with our other legal documents. It declares that Jane and I are both, equally, the official parents of Hannah Elisabeth Klempnauer Miller. We are a fact. We are a family.

[IV]

I lie with Hannah in our bed early in the morning. Jane has just finished nursing her and is off to take a shower. Hannah stretches her arms over her head, extending her body, almost willing it to grow. She is like a blade of grass, but a fat one, reaching up toward the sun. Her grabby hand lunges at my face. I've got to do something about her fingernails, but I can barely see their tiny tips well enough to clip them. She seizes my lip and holds on, ferret claw. I pry her fingers off. Next, she reaches toward my head and grabs a fistful of hair. She grins and gurgles. I raise my head and peer into her face. She looks at me, first as though she is reminding herself of who this monster is, and then, with the glee of recognition. She squints her eyes, a little wrinkle forming on the bridge of her nose. Her toothless, triangular mouth pops open. She chortles. This is my little girl, my lollipop, my daughter.

SIX

Mommy and Me

[1]

FOR TEN WEEKS, the three of us huddle together, like birds in a nest. Jane nurses Hannah and then nurses her again. We worry about her. We kiss her. We gaze at her. We rarely go out, except to the grocery store or Target. We become strangely obsessed with Dr. Phil, tuning in every day as he dishes out advice. He does a show on the biggest mistakes parents make, and we watch with rapt attention, certain that we would never make those same errors. Of course, it's important to provide consistent, but not dictatorial discipline. Of course, we will not have a tantrum-throwing, headstrong child. But we watch, newbies that we are, secretly hungry for advice. We watch a show on people who desperately need to be the center of attention. Another on a woman who claims to be married to Mr. Cheap. Another on women who dislike other women. Another on a father wracked with guilt over the death of his son. Every day, I find myself waiting for Dr. Phil, enjoying the vicarious emotional release of a stranger's personal struggle, at least until the next set of ads. Dr. Phil brings controlled drama to our lives. Instead of worrying about whether Hannah is constipated, I can worry about whether Mr. Cheap will ever take a financial laxative, or whether Jason's poor suffering father will ever be able to forgive himself.

And then, in the eleventh week, Jane goes back to work. This has an effect on her that is roughly equivalent to being slammed face first into the side of a cliff. In the morning, Jane feeds Hannah, gets dressed, packs up her briefcase, lunch, and breast pump, kisses Hannah, and leaves. In the afternoon, she returns, every particle of energy sucked out through her pores. She drops her breast pump on the chair by the door, picks up Hannah, and immediately sits down on the sofa to nurse. When she tells me about work, it is in sentences that are weighted down, as if they are tied to blocks of cement and facing the end of the pier. She cried again in her office, she tells me. She is exhausted, she tells me. She put her head down on her desk and fell asleep.

The truth is, I have no idea how to respond. My immediate response is guilt. I feel guilty for being at home. Jane feels guilty for not being at home. I feel guilty for not making money. Jane feels guilty for going to work. What would Dr. Phil say? You can't go through life with sweaty palms?

After years of living parallel lives, Jane and I have suddenly diverged. She is back in the world, although she doesn't really want to be there. I am in an environment so closed it is like a snow globe, but—mostly—I don't want to leave. She forces herself to worry about meetings and office politics. I spend my time warming bottles and doing dishes. Both of these lives seem off-kilter, as though our inner pendulums have gotten stuck at the top of their swings.

I decide that it might be time to take on some freelance work, a prospect I had left open with my office before Hannah's birth. I arrange a meeting to talk about what they may have for me. I find myself looking forward to the day, to putting on professional clothes, to talking about projects that have a clear start- and end-point. When I arrive, I say hello to people I have not seen since the pre-birth days. We chat: How's Hannah? Do you have a picture? And then, it's always the women who ask, "Are you bored?"

No, I say, I'm not bored.

I don't think I am.

Am I?

Should I be?

My day goes something like this: Hannah starts thumping her legs against her crib mattress around 5:30 a.m. I go into the nursery, lift her from the crib, change her, and carry her into the bedroom while she dives repeatedly at my breast, hoping beyond hope to draw milk through the pajama top and out of my dry nipple. I hand her to Jane and Hannah gets down to business. While she nurses, I take a shower and eat breakfast.

Jane showers, gets dressed, and leaves for work. Hannah and I stand at the front window, waving at the car and watching until Jane turns the corner and drives out of sight. Hannah sits in her bouncy seat or lies on a blanket on the floor. I empty the dishwasher. Make the bed. Maybe put some laundry in the washer. I listen to public radio.

Hannah is usually mellow in the morning. She dozes, then wakes and lies around, batting at her toys. I make lunch, which I will take to Jane's office, and put it in the refrigerator.

Hannah and I chatter for a while, me trilling my tongue and she concentrating on working her lips into shape to gurgle back. Maybe we go for a walk. If it is a rainy day, she falls asleep. If I am lucky, I get some time to write. Midmorning, she is hungry. Sometimes she is voracious. If I make a small bottle, she wants a second. If I have made a larger bottle, she is picky and will only suck a little. She is a tease.

We sit on the futon on the enclosed porch, the windows open to the morning. At the tender age of three months, Hannah has developed her first crush: on the ceiling fan. She flirts with it, her slow grin opening into a wide smile, a rapid turn of her head into my chest, and a coy look back. The fan is still turning; she's still in love. Sometimes, but only occasionally, she bursts into a full, rollicking belly laugh while watching the fan. This little baby, mouth open in an upside-down triangle, guffawing. This is her fan club. She is a fan fan.

Jane and I agreed that I would bring Hannah to her office at lunch throughout the summer so that she could nurse. At about 11:15, we get ready to go. I pack the diaper bag and the sandwiches I made earlier, along with some chips or fruit or leftover pasta salad. Hannah is ready to eat again. She sucks her hand, spit running down her wrist. I put her into her car seat. She begins to whimper. I carry her to the car and snap her carrier into the base in the back seat. The whimper gets louder. I get in on the driver's side, turn the ignition, and pull out of the driveway. By the first stoplight, she's wailing. "Hannah, we're going to see Mommy," I say. She doesn't care. "You're going to eat really soon." But soon is not now. Soon is never. I try singing. I sing "You Are My Sunshine," but I have to stop because I choke up every time I get to the part about not taking my sunshine away.

I switch to the "Alphabet Song." Hannah wails through it all, reaching a crescendo of screeching and gasping by the time we make it to S. She sounds as if she will choke on a sob. I remind myself that I read somewhere that no child has ever hurt herself crying. I wonder if it's true.

Red light. Slow traffic. When we are moving again, I go as fast as I can through the side streets. Hannah seems soothed by driving more than forty miles per hour. I know the speed limit is twenty-five. I don't care. I imagine being stopped by a police officer for breaking the speed limit. In my mind, I invite the police officer to sit inside our closed car with the wailing Hannah before deciding if I really deserve a ticket.

Finally, we get there. Jane is waiting outside her building. She is as eager to feed as Hannah is to eat. Jane gets in the car and attempts to soothe Hannah.

"Don't bother," I say. "Food is the only consolation." We drive to a park beside the Mississippi River, the main virtue of which is proximity. I pull up next to the garbage dumpster, which is the only unoccupied spot I can find. This will do.

Jane releases Hannah from her car seat and holds her to her swollen breast. Hannah latches on like a thirteen-pound piranha, smacking her insistent lips. She shudders and gasps, still caught in the grasp of her tears. She pants against Jane's breast. Suck, suck, gasp.

Once Hannah has recovered herself, Jane and I sit in the car with her and the three of us eat lunch. We take a walk through the park. A couple of college students are throwing a Frisbee. The Mississippi River moves its mud steadily and slowly downstream. A crow caws in a tree.

I drive Jane back to her office and Hannah and I head toward home. Sometimes, we stop on the way for a walk. I push her in her stroller, pausing when I hear birds singing. I talk to her about whatever crosses my mind: the weather, what we ate for lunch, the kids who are riding their bikes ahead of us, the names of the local lakes: Harriet, Hiawatha, Nokomis, Calhoun, Sunfish, Elmo, Isles. I sing little songs to her, some old, some that I just make up on the spur of the moment. Hannah, my peach, you are my peach.

At home, we settle in to read some stories. I read *I Love You As Much* and *The Big Red Barn*, pointing out all the different animals in each. Then it's naptime. I rock Hannah in the glider in her room, singing my playlist of hymns to her. They are soothing, they are long enough to get her to sleep, and they are just about the only songs to which I can remember all the words. *"Love will guide us. Peace has tried us. Hope inside us will lead the way."*

She falls asleep and I place her, as delicately as a glass egg, in her crib. She rustles, and I hold my breath, willing her to keep sleeping. She does. I slip into the other room. I lie down and nap, or I read, or I sit at my computer and do some work.

When Hannah wakes up, I give her a bottle and then we go for a walk around the neighborhood, stopping to look at the still-blooming lilacs. I hold her up so she can smell them and feel the blooms tickle her face. When we return, I pull her bouncy seat to the kitchen and set her in it. I make dinner, chatting a steady narration of what I'm doing. "This is a knife, Hannah. It's sharp, so it's only for Mama. This is a carrot. We'll be having carrots and meatloaf tonight. Well, you won't. At least, not directly."

When dinner is pulled together, we play. I move her arms and legs, jiggle toys, show Hannah her face in a mirror. She begins to get hungry. I try to fend her off so that Jane can nurse her when she gets home. Hannah does not approve. She begins to fuss and then cry. I bounce her. We stand by the window and watch for Jane's car. We go out into the yard and walk around, looking at leaves and flowers. Hannah hates me. I am cruel and malicious. I am starving her. I sing again. We go back inside.

Finally, Jane arrives. She looks exhausted but relieved to be home. She dumps her breast pump bag on the floor, hands me a couple of bottles of pumped milk to put in the refrigerator, and takes Hannah. They move like a unit to the sofa, where Jane unbuttons her shirt, pops open her bra, and begins to nurse. Hannah slurps and gurgles.

When she is done, Jane and I eat dinner. Then Jane lies on the floor with Hannah and plays with her, blowing little raspberries on her fat thighs. After a while, it's time to give Hannah her bath. Jane has decorated Hannah's white plastic bathtub with blue and red and yellow nonslip stickers cut into the shapes of animals. Hannah's name is spelled out in stickers across the middle of the tub. I set the tub on the bathroom counter and, using the pitcher from the coffee maker, fill it with warmish water. I set out the all-in-one baby wash, a cup to rinse her with, and two washcloths. For weeks, Hannah loathed her bath until an older mom told us she was probably screaming because she was cold. Now, we cover her torso with a washcloth soaked with warm water. She lies there happily, her wet hair slicked back, her round face glowing like the moon.

After the bath, Jane cuddles Hannah, who is wrapped in a yellow ducky towel, puts a diaper on her, and suits her up in a sleeper. Bedtime is nursing time again. Contrary to all good advice, we are allowing Hannah to fall asleep at the breast, her hand wound in Jane's hair. She drifts off around seven-thirty. Jane emerges from Hannah's room and collapses on the couch. She looks as though she has been caned. If she talks about work at all, her face is hard and closed. Sometimes she goes right to bed; sometimes she watches a little television and then goes right to bed. I go to bed pretty shortly thereafter. If we're lucky, Hannah will sleep until midnight. If we're really lucky, she will fall back to sleep quickly after her nighttime nurse without needing to be rocked or walked around her room. If we're insanely lucky, she'll continue to sleep again until she wakes at five-thirty. Then, repeat.

Am I bored? Do I miss my job? Not exactly, but I do miss the identity that went with it. Now that I am home all the time, I feel a need to prove that being at home is a job unto itself. I feel compelled to show that I am a worthy homemaker. I clean. A lot. I clean the bathroom, pick lint off the basement carpet, do laundry and more laundry, dust the living room, mop the kitchen.

I find myself becoming rigid to the point of rigor mortis about how things should be done around the house. Jane's cereal bowl was left on the counter? My God, woman, the dried-on granola bits are impossible to get off. Jane left the bag of bread sitting open on the kitchen counter? Fine, maybe I'll just leave it there and let the whole loaf go dry. That will show her.

"For God's sake," Jane says with exasperation. "You don't have to be June Cleaver."

But I feel like this is my new job. I want to show that I am not slacking. I want to exorcise some of the guilt I feel for not working when I know that work is draining Jane. I want to have a realm that I control. If I am not June Cleaver, in her apron and earrings, or my own mother, in her bathrobe and sleep-smudged mascara, who am I?

[11]

Jane and I have nothing to talk about anymore except Hannah. We talk about whether she seems healthy, if she's gassy, and when she last wet her diaper. We talk about her drool, her obsession with the ceiling fan, and how many bottles she's taken. We talk about whether she's too hot or too cold, how beautiful she is, how much she's growing.

But we don't talk about anything else. When I take Hannah to see Jane for lunch, I update her on our morning, and then we sit in silence.

"Why don't you bring a book?" Jane says one day. The next day, I pull a book out of the lunch bag after the turkey sandwiches and potato chips. Jane positions Hannah for nursing and I open my book, an anthology of essays about new motherhood. Jane looks a little abandoned.

"Do you want to talk?" I ask her.

"I don't have anything to say," she says with a shrug and gazes down at Hannah, who is sucking noisily.

We used to have everything to say. We used to talk to each other about every thought, every idea that passed our way. We talked about our dreams and our fears and our hopes and our frustrations. We talked about stories we heard on public radio and articles we read in the *New Yorker* and work and meetings and committees and home repairs and friends. We never shut up.

Somewhere along the line, though, our conversations changed. They became less about ideas and more about emotions, less excitement and more process. Some of this is marriage and some of it, I have to admit, is lesbianism, given our affinity for processing to death. I don't know why this happens; maybe it is the inevitable result of generations of female socialization. Or maybe it is all that estrogen under one roof. Whatever the reason, lesbians can spend years, literally, talking about our childhoods. We can emote on demand. Not all lesbians do this, but certainly enough do to justify the stereotype.

There was a certain safety in the midst of all our processing. I liked the attention that came with it. I liked the fact that Jane is naturally nurturing, so she was instinctively inclined to ask me how I felt, and then to listen. I liked the affirmation that, nine times out of ten, accompanied a good processing session.

"I miss our time alone," I say one evening as we collapse on the sofa after finally getting Hannah to sleep.

"Uh-huh," Jane says, "but I don't miss all of the hours that we spent talking about our relationship."

She doesn't? On one level, I'm not surprised. I know I can be—how do I put this?—high-maintenance. I know that I withdraw when I am upset, that I let anger fester. I know that my temper is short and, these days, getting shorter. In the pre-Hannah past, Jane often took on the task of drawing me out, talking me down, leading me back to the world. At least part of me wants her to keep doing that. But she's flat-out too tired. Fine, I think. I don't need it anyway.

[I I I]

On Saturday morning, we go to the Farmer's Market. I love it here: the air laden with the rich smells of cilantro and beans and basil and onion. The dirt still clinging to vegetable roots. The wealth of fresh food just pulled from soil. It brings me no end of pleasure that

Hannah adores it, too. We navigate our way through the narrow aisles stuffed with people carrying scallions and bread and flowers and eggs. Strapped into her Baby Bjorn and hanging from my chest like an unwieldy appendage, Hannah waves her arms and kicks her feet with the sheer joy of it all.

I love to carry Hannah through the crowd, her little bottom pressed against my stomach, her fingers grasping the air. I love kissing the top of her head, encased in its pink cotton hat. I even love the feeling of her heels pummeling my abdomen when she gets excited. And I like the attention that we get from other people. I ask Jane if it bothers her that I carry Hannah so much. "Nope," she says. "I carried her for nine months."

We stop at one of the stands to buy scones and coffee for breakfast. The woman behind the table grins and waves at Hannah, then looks at me and asks, "Is she your first?"

"Yes," I say, because she is and because I am her mother, in fact and in principle, but I feel as though I should stop the conversation and explain. She is my first, but I didn't bear her. I am her mother, but there is another.

I feel like I'm somehow cheating. If I am carrying the baby, Jane disappears. Hannah is the center of attention, followed by me, because I am the one to whom she is strapped. Jane becomes a fifth wheel, a friend or an aunt. People look at me and assume, naturally, that I am the natural mother—that is, the birth mother. This is what some women mean when they say that parenthood erases lesbians. Even those who look stereotypically butch are suddenly seen as apple-pie moms when carrying a baby. Maybe Jane and I should start kissing in public, I think. Or maybe we should hold hands everywhere we go. But then, who would carry the diaper bag?

Before Hannah was born, I thought that the best way to handle the whole question of lesbian parenthood was to treat it as though it is absolutely normal. In casual conversations and grocery store lines, I planned to interact with other people based on the assumption that our family is just the same as everyone else's, but different. We do, after all, live ridiculously normal lives, with our little suburban rambler and our frequent trips to Target to buy more Huggies. But of course, I know that our family is not the norm. Gayby boom notwithstanding, we are the exception.

When I call the doctor's office and talk about my daughter, they immediately assume that I am the birth mom. When I strap Hannah into the Baby Bjorn and run errands, people who admire her assume, naturally enough, that I am the stay-at-home mom while my husband is at the office. Even when the question doesn't come up, I feel as though I am somehow staying in the closet by not explaining myself.

The problem is that, to avoid future misunderstanding and embarrassment, I have to come out before I otherwise would. I don't begrudge the fact that people assume that I am straight. I certainly don't expect complete strangers to look at me and somehow recognize that I am a Sexual Minority. But it is nonetheless annoying. It means that I have to shine a preemptive spotlight on the way that I am different, on the way that our family is outside the norm. People ask what they consider an innocuous question and to answer it honestly, or at least to avoid confusion, I have to come out.

"Are you nursing?" I'm not, but my partner is. (We're gay.)

"She's beautiful. I bet Daddy's proud." Nope, but her other mommy sure is. (I'm gay.)

"Oh, she looks just like you." In fact, she looks nothing like me, but astonishingly like Jane, with the same espresso-colored eyes, the same downward turn at the corners of her mouth. I came across a picture of newborn Jane recently and thought at first that it was Hannah, so alike are they. Thank you, I think, but if you think she looks like me, you should see her birth mother.

[IV]

By midsummer, it is hot and rainy, the kind of rain that hangs in the air, part water, part vapor. I feel as though we are living in a teapot. It dripped all night and poured all morning. With the exception of a brief trip to the grocery store, I've been inside all day with the baby. We walk around the house. We walk around the house again. We look out the bedroom window at the wet yard. There's a world out there that I almost remember. I try to read a book to Hannah. It catches her attention for two thick, cardboard pages and then she begins to wail. I rock her. She wails some more. She wants to move around, or, more precisely, she wants me to move around, carrying her while I do my bouncy astronaut walk around the living room. I go into the kitchen and look at the clock. 1:42. Only four more hours until Jane gets home.

We go into the bathroom and look in the mirror. "Do you see the baby, Hannah?" I say. I have read that mirror play is engaging to babies. "Who's that baby? Who's that baby, Hannah? That's you, Hannah. You're the baby and I'm the mama." She couldn't care less. I check the clock. 1:47.

Back to the living room. I hold Hannah and bounce her up and down in front of the window. I think I'm going to die by two o'clock.

When I was a girl, I inhaled the *Little House on the Prairie* series, both in book and television form. I have reconnected with it recently because reruns of the TV series air every day at three o'clock, just about when I'm ready to hit the spit-up-covered wall. I used to identify most closely with Laura (who didn't?), but these days, I find myself thinking of Ma and the other poor pioneer women, stuck with a passel of kids and living like moles in sod houses dug into the Minnesota prairie. No wonder so many of them lost it.

• • •

Night comes, eventually. We have dinner, Jane nurses Hannah, Hannah falls asleep in her crib. The air has thinned and cooled markedly. I sit on the sofa, looking at the newspaper, listening for rustling from Hannah's room. Jane walks into the living room and examines the thermostat on the wall. She adjusts it, turning the air conditioning from frigid to arctic.

"My God, it's a sweat bath in here," she moans. She stands in front of me, like a turkey roasting in hormonal juices. She is dressed in shorts and a t-shirt, her hair pulled back off her face. I huddle on the couch in my sweatshirt, jeans, and fleecy socks.

"Couldn't we open the windows?" I ask. I want to let the warm, moonlit air into the house. "You have got to be kidding," Jane says. She goes to bed, although it is still early. I read the paper some more, herd the cats into the basement for the night, and walk into the bedroom. I hear a whirring sound. Jane has turned the portable fan to high and has it pointed directly at her. She lies on top of the blankets, her pajama shirt pulled up to her neck. She looks at me.

"I'm dying," she says.

"It's your hormones."

"It's stifling in here. You have to admit it."

I have to do no such thing. I have goose bumps. I pull a blanket off the bed and carry it into the living room where I curl up on the couch. The air conditioner chugs away. The moon peers through the window. The branches of the honey locust trees shift soundlessly in the night breeze, casting shadows on the wall.

"What's wrong?" Jane asks me a few nights later. She asks this a lot. About nine times out of ten, I answer, "Nothing." This drives her nuts.

She asks again.

What's wrong is that I don't know exactly what's wrong. I feel bad, defensive, quick to snap at Jane, kind of flat. This happens periodically and I generally am not aware of what precisely brings it on. Biorhythms? Menstrual cycle? Satan?

This evening, my focus is on my raging lack of intellect. I have made the mistake of reading the *New York Times Magazine*. Normally, this is not a problem, but this week, it included an article that criticized some author for being intellectually soft and unsophisticated. If they are unsophisticated, what am I? I'm not just unsophisticated; I'm naïve, plebeian, slow on my feet, unemployed, out of it.

I'm a stay-at-home mom. I feel out of it because I am out of it.

As I'm getting ready for bed, I realize that part of the problem is that I miss working. That is not to say that I miss my job, which I don't. I don't miss my job; I miss working.

The air conditioning is again running full blast, so I pull on my navy flannel pajamas with the snowflake print. I throw my socks at the laundry basket. One misses. I toss my shirt with the dried, sour spit-up on the right arm after them. I miss brain activity, the grown-upness and focus that are part of the work world. I still get some of it, but only when Hannah is asleep. Mostly, I stay in the shallow end of the intellectual pool, where I can get out quickly if she needs me. There is little time to swim into deep water, roll over, and float.

I pad into the bathroom and look in the mirror as I floss my teeth. Maybe my problem is that I'm not smart, I think. Or maybe it's a lack of drive. Or—here's a good one—it's a dearth of confidence. I can be insecure for hours about my lack of confidence. I believe, like the Tin Man or the Scarecrow or the Lion, that any of these things—brains or drive or spirit—would make me feel better, think better, work better. I would be more productive. I would write more. I would be published in something other than newspapers that are handed out for free. My work would be more cogent. It might be, even, sophisticated.

Or maybe not.

[V]

Jane, meanwhile, is depressed. Usually, depression is my territory, so the role reversal feels strange. It started when she went back to work. It slipped into the house like an odorless, but toxic, vapor and has continued ever since, ebbing and flowing with a cycle known only to itself. Jane is growing used to its presence. She is getting to know its rhythms and says that she can tell when the darkness is about to descend.

I have rarely seen Jane depressed, so it's hard for me to measure its magnitude. Is this mild? Is it severe? I console myself that she doesn't have anything like the symptoms that show up in the newspaper: the postpartum woman who suddenly snaps and pitches her baby over the edge of a bridge. Jane is exhausted, demoralized, exhausted, weepy, exhausted, impatient, exhausted.

At the end of the workday, Jane comes home and, as usual, drops her purse and breast pump on the dining-room table. She goes immediately to Hannah, picks her up, and kisses her. Holding the baby, Jane is suddenly light and exhilarated. She coos to Hannah and settles in to nurse. She holds onto Hannah like a buoy.

We eat dinner, and then Jane plays with Hannah on the blanket that is spread in the middle of the living-room floor. She shakes rattles and talks to her about the pictures in a board book. Hannah smiles and gurgles and rolls around until it's time for bed. Jane carries Hannah into the nursery to change her into a sleeper. She brings her back out into the kitchen, where I am putting dishes into the dishwasher. "Say good-night, Mama," she says. I kiss Hannah once on each cheek. Jane takes her back into the nursery.

Once Hannah is asleep, Jane comes back to the living room and, as usual, collapses on the sofa. She looks like she has not slept in days. She descends with each minute. Her eyes glaze.

"How was your day?" I ask.

"It sucked."

"Did something happen?"

"Just the usual crap. Stupid stuff. I have a ton of stuff to do and I'm not getting to it. I cried again. Pretty much a typical day."

Jane's eyes droop and begin to squint. The muscles in her face hang slack. I really have no idea what to do, but I feel like I should do something. I want to make the problem go away.

"Why don't you go to bed?" I say. This isn't a good idea. She looks defensive, as though I am criticizing her.

I try again. "Do you want to talk?"

"I feel like I'm not doing anything well," she says. She looks limp, piled into a ball in the corner of the sofa. "I'm not a good employee. I'm not a good partner. I'm not a good mother."

"You're doing great," I say. She looks at me as though I'm crazy. "You've got a ton on your plate right now and you're totally exhausted. Why don't you go to bed?"

"I can't. I have to pump."

"Then go pump. Go downstairs, watch television, pump, and then go to bed."

"Don't pressure me."

I am frustrated. I want my Jane back, my capable, stable Jane. I don't know what to do with Jane depressed. And the truth of the matter is that depression scares me—in myself, in Jane, in anyone, to be perfectly honest. My inclination is to run away or, failing that, to impose order on it. Neither of these responses is even remotely helpful.

"Do you want me to come downstairs with you?" I ask.

She looks at me, a fleeting glimmer of herself. "Would you?"

SEVEN

Words

[I]

I AM LEARNING HANNAH'S LANGUAGE. AN agitated "ming ming" means she's hungry. A sudden shriek means she is in pain. When she is angry, she goes rigid, her face suddenly narrow and hard, red as fire, tears squeezing from her eyes like lemon juice. She pulls on her left ear when she is thinking about food.

When Hannah is not talking to me, I am talking to her. I keep up a running narrative of just about everything. I tell her what I'm doing. I tell her where we're going. I sing her little songs. The truth is that over the past several years, I have become more of a self-talker anyway, so it's refreshing to finally have an audience, if one that is strapped to my chest. Just being there, Hannah makes me look not only less weird, but outright nurturant.

Twice each day, at naptime, our conversation turns to song. To slide Hannah into sleep, I sing quietly, my lips touching the fluffy hair that sprouts from her head like spring grass. Without thinking, I turn to hymns because they are the songs I grew up with, the songs I remember, the songs that I have heard and sung so many times over so many years.

I grew up in church, metaphorically and literally, spending thousands of hours at Sunday services, in church school, at Vacation Bible School, at Methodist Youth Fellowship. I even occasionally went to the church with my father on off-hours. He would work in his office; I would do homework in the sanctuary. I loved the church, until I didn't, until I discovered in early adulthood that congregations are just as human and just as fallible as any other organization, despite all the lofty talk. Like others who grew up in ministerial families, my adulthood has been dominated by a love-hate relationship with church, but I still unequivocally love hymns. They are the music of my childhood. When I was eight and nine years old, I would lie in bed at night and serenade myself with music from the bright red United Methodist hymnal with the embossed golden cross and flame on the cover. "Holy, Holy, Holy." "We Gather Together." "They'll Know We Are Christians by Our Love." I put myself to sleep this way, protected by the music's spell. I still sing hymns because they make me feel safe. I hope they will do the same for Hannah.

I do recognize the irony in our hymn-sing, though, because these days I am only a lukewarm believer in God. I have long thought that I have something of a faith deficit. I want to know outcomes. I want certainty. I want answers, not ambiguity. Faith feels inherently ambiguous to me, although I suppose that if I really had it, it would feel anything but. The truth is that I'm not even sure what faith is. I think of it as a sense, a sensation. Maybe it is like feeling full after eating. Maybe it is the sense of having answers in the midst of muddle. Is it hope? Is it the thing with feathers? Is it a groundedness in doctrine? Is faith itself a kind of deficit—a lack of doubt or skepticism? I think it must be something that you have or you don't. I imagine it as a character trait, like optimism. Maybe, I think, that's my problem.

Now that we have a baby, I find that the stories and assurances I learned as a child come flooding back: God is in His heaven, all's right with the world. Jesus loves you, this I know. Angels watch over you and guide your feet. If I should die before I wake, I pray the Lord my soul to take. The memory of my eight-year-old self still clings to these, like incantations. But my adult self rebels. Some form of reincarnation, cosmic recycling that it is, makes more sense to me than heaven. I doubt the reality of a personified God. I don't think that God is making decisions about what will happen in the world, or that God determines who will live and who will die, who will eat and who will not. I am not at all convinced that Jesus was divine, and I'm not sure about that whole resurrection thing, except very metaphorically. Oddly, I feel more open to angels because I am inclined to believe that spirits continue in some form and that they just might walk around in the world. I very rarely pray, though I am secretly convinced that it would be good for me.

I think I must be religiously challenged. Even though I have stood in churches all my life and have a master's degree in theology from a Christian seminary, I am stymied about what I want to teach my daughter about God and faith and church. I turn to the traditional liturgy of hymns, hoping on some level that they will provide comfort to Hannah now but won't have to be undone and deconstructed later.

And so, in the midst of this, we decide to have Hannah baptized. I am not entirely sure why we decide to do this. It may just be the force of tradition, or lingering superstition, or the sticky residue of faith. But both Jane and I want to have her baptized, partly for the symbolism of it all, partly because it seems like the thing to do, and partly to cover all the bases. If it turns out that all the talk about Heaven is right, and that you really can't get in without having had the drops of holy water applied to your forehead, I don't want to leave Hannah knocking at the pearly gates.

We want to have the baptism done at the church we have attended—more or, recently, less regularly—over the past nine years. The church is housed in a falling-down former warehouse on a falling-down street in Minneapolis. It has its own loading dock in the sanctuary, which the congregation cheerily refers to as a choir loft. At a United Church of Christ congregation, most of the people who attend on Sunday are gay and lesbian, with a few transgender folks and the occasional straight "ally" mixed in. The church, like the baptism itself, is a repository of ambivalence for me. For almost a decade, Jane and I have loved this church and it has driven us both nuts. All that gay and lesbian energy in one old warehouse fuels a love affair with drama and a near obsession with self-reflection. Sunday services are vibrant and powerful and creative and intimate. Outside of Sunday mornings, committees, subcommittees, task forces, teams, and liaisons are ubiquitous. Post-Its and pages torn from flip charts litter the walls. Worship–by-committee dominates the planning of services for every season of the year. Task forces hold listening sessions on this topic or that one. Virtually every meeting opens with a "check-in," during which each person in the room meanders through the events, ideas, issues, feelings, or concerns of the days since the last meeting. But then, when this congregation is not pouring its energy into creating new liturgies or new personnel policies or hashing and rehashing the best way to welcome new people, it turns its energy on itself, descending into self-mutilation, like a nervous and abused dog, chewing old wounds open again and again.

Jane and I are moving, slowly but steadily, toward the exit, but we don't have a connection yet with any other church. And, at the moment, we have baptism on our minds.

We talk with the minister, Rebecca, about our desire to baptize Hannah. It turns out that the two other lesbians from our childbirth education class, also members of this church, want to have their son, Lucas, baptized too. We decide to have a double baptism, kind of like a double wedding, but smaller. Because it is the church that it is, planning the baptism requires several meetings. We discuss why we want to have the children baptized. We discuss what baptism means (no washing away of sin here; our baptism will be about bringing the children formally into the community of God). And we discuss how it will be done. Then, because we couldn't possibly use the text that is printed in the back of the hymnal, we get down to the business of writing the liturgy.

On the day of the baptism, Jane, Hannah, and I show up early. Despite all our work to redefine this moment in a way that suits our liberal, modern sensibilities, tradition still tugs at us. Jane and I have felt an almost visceral need to formalize the event. This is a church where corduroys are considered dressy, but we spent hours looking for just the right outfit for Hannah. We didn't want the kind that made her look like a tiny bride, so we have her all decked out in a red, embroidered velvet dress, white tights pulled over her fat diaper, and tiny patent leather shoes on her feet. Shortly after we arrive, Lucas is carried in by his moms. He looks ethereal, dressed in a traditional white baptismal gown.

We sit in our folding chairs during the first half of the service. Hannah spends her time taking her shoes off her feet and shoving them in her mouth. Jane spends her time worrying about the chemicals in patent leather. I spend my time taking each shoe out of Hannah's mouth and returning it to her foot. She takes it off again.

At the appointed time, the six of us go to the front of the sanctuary, along with the friends and family whom we have asked to be there. Our friend, Mark, and my sister, Stace, are with us. Lucas's aunt and uncle stand with his mothers.

Jane and I promise to teach Hannah the stories, beliefs, and rituals of Christianity while encouraging her to respect and learn about the religious and spiritual traditions of others. We promise to help Hannah grow in spirit. We promise to nurture her wonder and curiosity. We promise to help Hannah discover hope and humor in the world, even in hard times. We promise to try our best to model fairness and respect. We promise to help Hannah feel embraced by the community of the Church.

Mark and Stace promise to love, respect, and protect Hannah, and to play with her, read with her, eat with her, help her find answers to her questions, and help her discover the world. They promise to lead and follow her, helping her to discern her own spiritual path as a beloved child of God. And the congregation, this congregation that we are at the moment holding on to by the tips of our fingers, promises to encourage Hannah's spiritual life and growth.

Rebecca takes Hannah in her arms and pours water over her forehead. She says a prayer. Hannah squirms and cries, grabbing for her shoe.

Afterward, I am glad that we have chosen to baptize Hannah. It feels like we have done the right thing, and an important thing, although I am not entirely certain what this thing is that we have done.

I do think it is good, but still, it has not brought clarity. Hannah is baptized, but still I do not know what I want to teach her about this whole faith thing. She's just six months old, so, presumably, we have some time to figure it out, but sooner or later Jane and I will need to talk with her about things religious. I am reluctant to give her the conventional picture of God that I absorbed as a child: half old man on the throne, half Santa Claus. And the truth is, I am reluctant to promote the idea of a Father God to a little girl with two mothers. If she learns the idea of a Father in Heaven, will she somehow think that her family is deficient? Would offering Hannah a Father God communicate to her that the gender of the parent matters more than the love of the parent?

But my own theology, such as it is, is vague and slippery. Can I tell her what I think I really believe—that God is the force that makes all life grow? Can I tell her that God is the spirit of love? Can I tell her that God is light? Wind? Air? Water? Breath? Wonder?

What I hope is to give Hannah some access points to faith that she won't feel she needs to undo when she grows up. I grew up praying to God the Father in Heaven, but I no longer feel that I can pass that faith along in any form other than metaphor. What I believe now is more like this: God is life. I would like Hannah to have a sense of God that embraces her like the noonday sun. I would like her to know that she is beloved, deeply and preciously. I would like her to know that God lives in beauty. The closest I seem able to come to that sense these days is through music. So I sing hymns.

On the night of Hannah's baptism, I walk back and forth on the blue-and-green rug in her room, carrying her in my arms and singing. Hannah relaxes. She's easing up to sleep. Although it is warm outside on this September evening, I segue into my Christmas repertoire, starting with my favorite, "What Child Is This?" I move on to "Silent Night," half in English and half in semi-remembered German. Hannah's thumb finds its way into her mouth. She softens.

I set her down gently in the crib and am slapped by her cry. She is decidedly not ready. I pick her up and begin to sing again, returning to my standby, the blessedly long "Love Will Guide Us." As always, I am caught off guard by the words, although I have sung them innumerable times.

> Love will guide us. Peace has tried us. Hope inside us will
> lead the way.
> On the road from greed to giving, love will guide us through
> the dark night.

This is the point, I think. Love will guide us. Hold my baby close and sing to her about love and peace and hope in a world that downplays all three. Listen to the words, and maybe I will come to believe in them myself.

[11]

Hannah and I have come to our first baby storytime at our suburban library. The reading room is full of children and mommies and the occasional nanny. Most of the twenty or so babies are crawling or walking, which seems to be a revelation to six-month-old Hannah. I think I should take her out more.

The librarian leading the half-hour session is a middle-aged woman named Barbara. She looks and acts like my fantasy of the perfect kindergarten teacher. Barbara is plump, with her hair cut into a practical bob. She wears not only sensible shoes, but sensible clothes. She is expressive and enthusiastic and eager to dance. Each of us is wearing a name tag with our name and the name of our child. Barbara, who holds a fluffy, white stuffed bear instead of a baby, wears a name tag that reads: Barbara and Bear.

Barbara opens with a song. I realize that I am one of only a few newcomers to this group, because most people here obviously know all the words. But it's a simple song and Barbara, in her kindergarten style, is easy to follow. Hannah stares at her with round eyes and gaping mouth.

We sing more songs and listen to three short stories that sneak in like interlopers. The parents all have a copy of each book to show to the children as Barbara reads. Hannah loves the books, but mainly as chew toys. We sing again, this time about two little blackbirds sitting on a hill, one named Jack and the other named Jill. And about shaking out our wiggles, and our ten little fingers, and the wheels on the bus that obsessively drives all over town. Hannah spills out of my lap and lies on her stomach on the floor, trying to gnaw the books in our pile. When I move them, she wriggles over to the next baby's books, mouth open.

At the end of the session, Barbara brings out a plastic tub of toys—mostly homemade shakers filled with rice and colorful bits of confetti—for the children to play with. The parents sit or stand in small groups, watching the kids and chatting. I introduce myself to a couple of the women, using my usual opener: How old is your little one? The conversations never seem to get past the exchange of our babies' ages. I try to leech onto a conversation that two women sitting near the toy tub are having, but they are both pregnant and busy discussing ultrasounds. I have little to add. I have no ultrasound pictures because I had no ultrasounds because I never got pregnant. My attempts at friendly eye contact get me nowhere.

By now, many of the parents have moved out of the reading room to pick out books from the low, child-sized shelves. The sole dad who came to storytime is standing by a bookshelf. I throw my line into the water once again: So, how old is your little one?

"Just turned one year," he says. "And yours?"

"Six months," I respond.

"Great," he says. "We started coming here when my daughter was six months." He's talking! I feel like I have broken through the sound barrier.

"Yeah, I thought there were a lot of repeaters here when we started singing and everyone knew the words," I say. We chat for a few more minutes. He tells me that he sings "Ten Little Fingers" to his daughter when she gets fussy in the car. I make a mental note to try that one. Maybe it will work. We say good-bye, see you next time.

I feel like I've found a friend, someone I can sit with in the lunchroom. I don't know why I often find it easier to talk to men than to women, but it has happened again. One man in the room, and he's the one with whom I end up having more than a two-sentence conversation. I don't know if this guy is gay or straight—he's wearing a conventional wedding ring and chances are that he's just a sensitive stay-at-home dad. Do I gravitate toward him because he's just friendly? Or because I feel like an outsider among moms?

The truth is that even six months into this, I still feel like a dad in drag. I still feel like I need to explain the fact that I did not birth my baby. I still want to sit in the guys' section. This is not because I am butch, that's for sure. I'm not even remotely athletic. I am a disaster with power tools. I literally cannot hammer a nail straight. I scream when a mouse gets into the house. I am a disappointment to butch women everywhere. But I'm kind of inept on the femme side too. I rarely wear makeup. I have never known what to do with my hair. I don't share my emotions easily. I certainly don't put myself in the same category as heterosexual moms. I feel as awkward talking to most of these moms as I ever did talking to the popular girls in junior high. Or as awkward as I think I might have felt talking to them, had I ever tried.

In the world of moms, I still feel like I am passing. I am using Mommy English as a Second Language, always trying to think about what clause is supposed to come next and trying to remember my idioms. It's a real bucket of monkeys.

Is this all in my head? In truth, no one has ever asked me who Hannah's "real" mother is, nor has anyone suggested that my presence might be harmful to her. If anything, several straight women have vaguely indicated that having two mothers in the house must be nice because, they assume, there is more help. On one level, I know that I do, in fact, have a lot in common with other moms. I change diapers, clean up baby food, do dishes, and sing songs to my baby just as they do. But I also continue to feel just a little apart, as though we live in two worlds that speak the same language but are divided by dialect.

I am somewhere in between, in a category still undefined but increasingly shared by second moms and second dads across the country. I have heard some lesbians talk about "mom" and "co-mom," which sounds to me like pilot and co-pilot. Which sounds to me like First and Second, Real and Almost Real. I don't want to be a co-mom. I don't want to be the second-in-command. I want to be seen as a real mom and, far more important than that, I want to *be* a real mom.

During Jane's pregnancy, I was consistently surprised by how often I was asked by straight colleagues, friends, and even family members what Jane and I would call ourselves, as if having two parents of the same gender would present a naming problem so formidable that we might just have to give up the whole idea of parenthood. The most common choice among the lesbian couples we know is to use Mom and Mama. We know a few other couples who have been more creatively courageous, using Maya, Mimi, Mama Bear, and Mama Sue. We quickly ruled out any title that includes the name of an animal. We considered whether we might pick a name from another culture, but our strongest connection is to Germany and I flat out refused to spend the next twenty years of my life being called Mutter.

In the end, I decided to call myself Mama, while Jane is Mommy. It is a name I never used for my own mother, so it feels less loaded with maternal expectation. I can invest it with my own meaning and, no doubt, my own baggage. I don't know yet exactly what that meaning will be, and I'll let Hannah sort out the baggage later, but I think what I am reaching for in calling myself Mama is to be wholly Hannah's and yet true to myself. I am trying to find a space between the worlds of Mommy and Daddy where I can fit.

[I I I]

By eight months, Hannah is chatting to herself, to us, to the reflection in the window, to anyone who cares to listen. She skips from consonant to consonant, trying on one and then another. She curls the tip of her tongue against her upper lip. "La, la, laaaa." She digs through her toy basket, pulling out books and rattles and the hairbrush that she loves to suck. "Baaaaaaaa, ba." She looks up and gives Jane a six-tooth grin. "Ha-boo," she says.

For weeks, I have been trying to teach her to say "Mama." I narrate my activities throughout the day, always in the third person. "Mama is making you lunch, Hannah. Mama is cutting a pear for you. Mama is picking you up. Mama loves you." When I change her diaper, I lean over her face, repeating *ma-ma-ma-ma-ma-ma* like a mantra.

I have even tried to teach her "Mama" in baby sign language. We have, of course, bought a book on teaching sign to babies and I have read that some babies will use fifty, even a hundred signs. They use signs for airplane and bunny. For kitty and dog. For blanket. For bottle. For toy. The book offers a prescribed sign for "Mother" and one for "Father," but none—not surprisingly—for "Other Mother." So I make one up. I pat my cheek softly with the palm of my hand whenever I say "Mama." Hannah looks at me with interest and then moves her bunched fingers toward her mouth. Hungry. The sign for "Hungry," the sign for "Milk," and the sign for "More" are the only ones she has ever cared to use. The rest, apparently including "Mama," are irrelevant.

At long last, my efforts are rewarded. Hannah discovers the letter M and begins to mix "ma" among "ba" and "la" and "ga." "It doesn't mean anything yet," I tell Jane, although I desperately want it to mean something, everything. "She's just making sounds. The meaning comes later."

Hannah's babbling increases. She begins to use inflection as she chirps and chatters. I continue to talk about myself, patting my cheek the whole time. "Mama is getting you dressed, Hannah. Mama thinks you're very pretty." Pat, pat.

Meanwhile, Jane seems almost oblivious to my naming obsession. I find it annoying that Jane frequently confuses our names, calling herself both Mommy and Mama. I find it even more annoying that I sometimes do the same thing. I want Hannah to be clear about what our names are. Other lesbian parents have told me that their kids learn quickly who is Mama and who is Mommy. They draw a clear distinction and they learn to work it, specifying that they want to be put to bed by Mommy, not Mama, or dressed by Mama, not Mommy.

Hannah's not going to know, I think. Jane and I will just morph into one big maternal figure. Or, and this is what lingers in my thoughts like smoke, I'll be neither Mommy nor Mama. Jane will be both. I'll be the other. The live-in. The friend. The "aunt." The nanny.

At dinnertime, I wave a spoonful of strained apples and blueberries in front of Hannah's lips. "Mama is feeding you, Hannah. Can you say Mama? Mamamamamamama."

After dinner, I get ready to give Hannah her bath. I set the plastic baby tub in our bathtub. I get out the rubber duck, the washcloth, the baby shampoo, and the pink lamb-shaped sponge. I run the water and then go into the nursery to tell Jane that everything is ready. Jane is standing by the changing table, pulling Hannah's shirt off. Hannah shakes her head free. She opens her mouth in a wide smile and looks straight at me. "Da-da!" she says.

EIGHT

First Floor, Maslow's

[1]

"I HOPE YOU'LL WRITE MORE ABOUT JANE," a man in my writing group says. He looks dreamy. "About the sensuality of the milk-laden breasts."

Jane snorts when I tell her this. "They're udders," she says.

Jane is sitting on the floor in the basement, watching a nature show on PBS. Her shirt is pushed up to her neck. "Do you want to see where your daughter bit me?" she asks.

She holds two funnels, each attached to a bottle, one pressed against each breast. Clear plastic tubes twine down from the funnels to the motorized pump encased in the stylish black bag of her "Pump In Style." (Black, after all, goes with everything.) The pump exerts a rhythmic suction, pulling her nipples out and releasing, out and release. Her nipples look like Vienna sausages in the round funnels. Milk squirts into the bottles. Every so often, she leans forward and shimmies her shoulders and chest, encouraging any sequestered reservoirs to let loose.

Nursing is wonderfully effective at deglamorizing the breast.

Later in the evening, Jane and I lie in bed together, somehow not so exhausted that we fall immediately into sleep. I roll toward her and kiss her. She smiles and touches the side of my face. I lean into her. I pull the sheet up over my shoulders and reach under her flannel pajama top with the line drawings of cats printed all over it. I touch her nipple. I rub her breast. I close my eyes.

"Um, could you not do that?" Jane says. "It kind of hurts."

I roll onto my back. I am embarrassed and disappointed.

"I'm sorry, honey," she says. "I'm just really sore."

I say that I understand, which I do, in theory. I say that it's fine, which it has to be. I think about how beautiful nursing is.

One Friday afternoon, when Hannah was about five months old, Jane came home from work and deposited her pump case on the dining-room table. We had dinner on the porch. Jane put Hannah to bed as usual. Then she began to gather her equipment together to pump. "Oh my God," I heard her gasp. "Oh my God, oh my God." I went into the living room.

"What's wrong?"

"I can't find the cord for my pump," she said breathlessly. "Oh my God. I must have left it at the office." She ransacked the bag. "Maybe it's in the car," she said and ran to the garage to check. She came back empty-handed. "I left it at the office. I can't believe it. I have to go get it." Her voice was pitching into panic. "What am I going to do if I can't get in?"

Jane's office had been quarreling over security procedures for months and had just implemented tighter rules, which she had strongly advocated.

"Oh my *God*."

She threw on her shoes and ran out the door. An hour later, she was back, clutching the pump cord. Jane connected the bottles to the tubes to the pump to the cord to the wall. She settled herself in the blue chair in the living room and pulled up her shirt. She positioned the funnels against her breasts and adjusted the speed of the motor.

She looked up, blissfully relieved. "Honestly, I have no idea what I would have done," she said. "There was no way I could get through the whole weekend pumping manually." The manual pump that the hospital gave us is like a Barbie breast pump. It's like emptying a flooded boat by sucking out the water with a straw.

For months, I was jealous of Jane's ability to nurse. I wanted to know what it felt like, to have the chance to feel milk flowing from my body into a baby. I wanted to experience the intimacy of nursing. I wanted to feel my baby cuddled against my chest, drawing food from inside me.

And then there was the reality.

The propaganda of breastfeeding suggests that, while "it might take a little getting used to at the beginning," the process is intimate and soft and calming and delightful. New mothers and mothers-to-be are barraged with information about the nutritional value of breast milk and how nursing passes on essential immunities. Immediately after Hannah's birth, at least five different women worked with Jane on establishing a proper latch. I hovered at her side, monitoring Hannah's mouth to see if it was appropriately flanged. Everyone told Jane to relax.

In the early days, Hannah wanted to suck so much and, as it turned out, was getting so little, that Jane tried to nurse her at almost any point when they were both awake. Visitors came and went, at the hospital and, later, at our home. "Hope you don't mind," Jane said to whomever was in the room as she opened her shirt. She always tried to be discreet, but the fact is that discretion is difficult when you are trying to wedge your breast firmly into someone else's mouth.

Hannah was born hungry. The nurses at the hospital were pleased by her tiny jaws working up and down. When Jane woke up sufficiently from the anesthesia, a nurse wheeled her gurney from the recovery room to the Special Care Unit, where Hannah had been placed for a couple of hours of observation. Jane first saw her there, lying in the Isolette and sucking away on a pacifier. The nurse put Hannah on Jane's chest. "Here she is, Mommy," she said. Jane's face was wet with tears. She rubbed her nipple lightly at the edge of Hannah's mouth. Hannah, not wasting any time, opened her mouth wide and began to suck.

Because Jane had had a C-section, which confuses the milk-stimulating hormones, we knew that it would likely take a while for Jane's milk to come in. We didn't know it would take a full four days and that, even then, there would be a trickle where we expected a river.

Jane told the nurses that she wanted to feed Hannah "on demand," meaning that she would nurse whenever Hannah wanted to eat. Demand was high; supply was low. "Sometimes it takes a while," the nurses reassured us.

By the morning of day three, Hannah was mad. She would cry, Jane would hold her to the breast, and Hannah would flail her head back and forth. A little dribble of milk would show up at the corner of her lips. "You're doing great," the nurse said when she stopped by. "Just keep trying. The more she sucks, the more it tells your body to make milk." By midafternoon, Hannah was furious. The nurse suggested giving her a little glucose. She offered it to Hannah in an eyedropper. Hannah sucked it back like a starving puppy.

And then she began to vomit. Our three-day-old baby was vomiting sugar water, while Jane tried to will herself into making milk. We paged the nurse. "She'll be all right," the nurse said. "It just didn't agree with her. Here, why don't you try to breastfeed her?"

Jane did try. She tried and tried. That evening, we talked about the situation to the nurse on the night shift. "Why don't we give her a little formula?" she said, almost conspiratorially. "It won't hurt." She brought a few jars of prepared formula, along with some sterile medicine cups and eyedroppers. "Just like this," she said, and demonstrated by putting the dropper in the corner of Hannah's mouth and squeezing slowly. "You can offer her your finger to suck on, too, if that helps her take it." Jane held the baby and I fed her, alternating dropper, then pinky. Hannah sucked gratefully on both and then fell asleep in Jane's arms.

We had no idea how much to feed Hannah, how much she was

getting, or how much she should be getting. When she screamed and flailed, we gave her formula in an eyedropper. Meanwhile, Jane kept nursing.

When Hannah was one week old, we went to the pediatrician's office for a checkup. It was our first group venture out of the house. The nurse checked Hannah over, saying that everything looked good. She asked about breastfeeding. Jane said she was nursing twelve to fourteen times a day, which seemed to please the nurse. Then the nurse asked Jane to demonstrate. She peered at Hannah's mouth from all angles, checking to see if she was well latched, if her lips were open enough, if she was taking the full areola into her mouth. She made a few adjustments. "We don't want to let her be lazy," the nurse said. "That will just give you sore nipples." We were sent home.

The next week, we went back for our two-week checkup. Hannah had not yet climbed back up to her birth weight. She was gaining weight, but too slowly. The nurse was a little concerned. She asked again about nursing. "Are you drinking lots of water?" Jane said yes. "Are you getting rest?" No, we have a newborn. Finally, she asked Jane how many times Hannah sucked per swallow. "About three or four times, I guess," Jane said. "Ah, that's the problem," the nurse said. "It should be suck, swallow, suck, swallow. She's not getting enough milk. She's working too hard."

Jane looked as though she had just gotten a D on her report card. "What am I supposed to do?" she asked.

The nurse pulled out a prescription pad and scribbled a couple of things. "Go get some Mother's Milk tea and some fenugreek," she said. "Women have been using these things for hundreds of years. And drink more water. When you think you've drunk all you can, drink some more."

Jane began taking fenugreek, an herbal supplement, and drink-ing her Mother's Milk tea, which, like a witch's potion, had to steep for ten minutes. She had been warned that fenugreek would make her urine smell like maple syrup. Our bathroom began to smell like the International House of Pancakes. Slowly, but definitely, Jane's milk supply began to increase. She was ecstatic.

We went back to the pediatrician's office, at the request of the nurse, for a weigh-in. She wanted to see if Hannah had climbed back to her birth weight by the third week. In fact, she had a growth spurt, as if she had been holding back just to generate extra excitement. Jane was instructed to continue the fenugreek, and we were given official permission to continue supplementing nursing with formula.

Over the next several weeks, Jane gorged on fenugreek and Mother's Milk tea. She perpetually had a large glass of water by her side. She was all fluid. Hannah reveled in the increased milk supply, little streams of milk dribbling down her chin. We still occasionally supplemented with formula, but only when Hannah genuinely seemed hungry after cleaning Jane out.

After ten weeks of this, Jane went back to work, Pump In Style in hand. Almost immediately, her milk supply began to decline. She pumped multiple times during the day, but she often came home with just one or two small bottles to put in the refrigerator. She drank her water, ate her herbs, and drank her tea, but it was a force she could not overcome. It was as though her breasts, missing Hannah's ready presence, wilted.

And then, one morning, about two weeks after Jane returned to work, she noticed blood in Hannah's diaper. She called the nurse at the pediatric clinic, who set up an appointment.

"Looks like a dairy allergy," the doctor said after examining Hannah and Hannah's diaper. She told Jane to go off dairy products and to report back if the symptoms recurred. We went home. I know little about food allergies or, for that matter, food restrictions of any kind. I assumed that going off dairy basically meant no milk, no ice cream, and no yogurt.

At home, we had muffins made with buttermilk. Jane was not sure if she could eat one. They were baked; did that solve the problem? She called the nurseline. No buttermilk, she was told. How about a bagel? Not if it has dairy in it. Do bagels have dairy in them? Neither one of us knew for sure.

Within a few days, blood showed up in Hannah's diaper again and we headed back to the doctor's office, where we were told, by a different physician, that no dairy means *no dairy*. Hannah, it turned out, was reacting to the dairy proteins in Jane's milk. To get rid of the proteins, Jane could not ingest anything containing any kind of dairy product. This, we discovered, not only meant no milk or ice cream or yogurt, but also no whey. What's whey? The only thing I knew was that Miss Muffet ate it just before the scary spider appeared. In fact, it is the liquid left over after milk has been curdled and strained. Yum. We started to read labels, discovering that dairy in one form or another works its wily way into all kinds of foods, from crackers to salad dressing to cereal bars.

Jane sorted through her diet, eliminating all signs of the cow. It's funny what you miss. I would have assumed that ice cream, cheese, and milk would be the hardest things to give up, but it turns out that it's butter. Jane was frustrated by not being able to put butter on bread, not being able to fry an egg in butter, not being able to put butter on a potato. We found a vegan margarine at the food co-op, which was as close as we could come to the real thing, though its relation to butter was something like Muzak's relation to Brahms.

Jane was vigilant and Hannah showed no further signs of illness. Then one day, Jane ate an English muffin. Hannah again began to bleed. Not a lot—it was never a lot—but it was enough that Jane was ready to emotionally impale herself for eating without reading the ingredients first. There is whey in English muffins. It was the spider that sat down beside her.

We became extra vigilant. I spent Hannah's naptime on the

computer, searching for non-dairy recipes. In addition to eliminating dairy, Jane understandably did not want to eat foods that risked giving either her or Hannah stomach pains. This meant that cabbage was out (not that that was a great loss), as well as all its cabbage-like relatives. No broccoli. No onions or garlic. No bowls of beans. Forget the stir-fry. We turned to meat, eating chicken and pork chops and more chicken and sausage and ham. Jane does not eat beef, and hasn't for years, so that was off our list from the outset. I tried to rotate the meals: one poultry, one porcine.

Friends who eat normally did not understand this. When one friend invited us over for dinner, Jane spotted something suspicious in the spaghetti sauce. "Does this have cheese in it?" she asked. "Oh, don't worry," our friend said reassuringly. "There's just a little." Jane ate salad instead—no bread—carefully scanning the list of ingredients on each bottle of dressing for traces of milk.

Jane had set out with the best of nursing intentions. She planned to breastfeed for at least a year, pointing out that the World Health Organization even recommended continuing for two years "or beyond." But nursing has not agreed with her. Jane hates pumping. She suffers regular bites from Hannah, who of course, teethed early. She is aggravated that, despite her fenugreek habit, her milk flow has remained insufficient to meet Hannah's growing demand. And now, Hannah has become more and more crabby about any activity that restricts her view of the world. Over the past few weeks, Jane has begun to broach the subject of stopping earlier. She considers December, when Hannah will be nine months old. I am inclined to think that stopping is a good idea, mainly because of the array of inconveniences that have accompanied breastfeeding.

But still, there is the sweetness of holding baby to breast. And it is that sweetness that holds her back.

"What would you think if I didn't stop nursing in December?" Jane asks one evening.

"Are you serious?" I say.

"I'm just thinking. It's so good for Hannah."

"Do you want to keep nursing?" I ask.

Jane tilts her head and smiles, and I see that her mind is made up. "Well, you know, I kind of like it. I don't really want to quit."

In the end, it was Hannah who decided, which is probably a precursor of things to come. With each day, Hannah grew fussier about drinking from the breast, perpetually craning her head around to look in other directions. Hannah's no fool; she figured out quickly that bottles are mobile, while breasts are not. The breast lost to the bottle because the breast blocked Hannah's view of the world. And the world is where she wants to be.

[11]

When we are not worrying about feeding, we are fantasizing about sleeping. For a while, Jane and I were smug about Hannah's sleep patterns. Sleep problems were for other people's kids; our amazing baby slept on her own. At about six weeks, we moved her from our bed to her crib, clearing the weekend for the firestorm we had been told to expect. But nothing happened. She settled right in without a whimper. When we introduced a 7:00 p.m. bedtime, she stretched her arms and began to yawn and rub her eyes each night by 6:40. At five months, she slept through the night (through the real night, not the pediatrician's measure of five hours) for six nights in a row. Jane and I woke up rested and stunned.

And then we learned: God smites the smug.

Now, at ten months old, Hannah sits on my lap in the glider in her dark bedroom, wide awake at 2:00 a.m. She is curled up on my lap, leaning forward against my right arm. I am trying to be still and quiet, remembering the advice that a friend's mother gave to her after the birth of her first child: be as boring as possible at night. I focus on being boring. Hannah doesn't seem to notice. From time to time, she takes a deep breath and trumpets a flatulent and spitty raspberry into the crook of my elbow. She squirms. She lets out a cry. After about forty-five minutes of this, she settles down. I rub her back in soft, repetitive, lulling circles. I wonder what will happen if I fall asleep. Will I drop her? Will I care? I stare at her nightlight, its spotted cow suspended in midair, halfway over the moon.

Finally, she begins to doze. Slowly, slowly, I ease her onto her back, nestling her against my chest. She purses her lips, sighs, and reaches one hand toward my shoulder. I rock her. Gingerly, I stand up and move to the side of the crib where I stand, rocking her, for a few more minutes. Her breathing is soft and regular. She doesn't move. Her feet are limp.

I set her onto the mattress. She begins to roll onto her side—this is good—and then she stops. She notices that something is gravely wrong. She is not being held. There is a pause. And then she wails.

An offended baby is a dangerous thing. Hannah screams, building up to a full shriek. The crib is an abomination unto the Lord. It is torture. It is abandonment. It is the tenth level of hell.

I pick her up. Silence. She is the human version of a close-and-play record player, those orange plastic boxes from my childhood with the needle in the lid that scratched out the tune to "Tina the Ballerina." I put Hannah down. She bawls.

I pick her up again and return to the glider. She nestles her head against my shoulder. I may be forgiven. But only if I am good.

I could live with this pattern when it only occurred once a night. But around seven months, when the sleep books that we have collected say that "most" babies are sleeping through the night, she began to wake at ten thirty and eleven thirty and twelve thirty, with a climax of screaming at about two o'clock. I pick Hannah up, and she's blissful. I put her down, and it may as well be on a bed of spikes.

I cannot take it any more. I feel like I am a nighttime hostage, held by a sadistic keeper who will not let me sleep more than fifty minutes at a time. Jane and I try to divide the night, as the books helpfully suggest, but it just means that we are both exhausted in the morning.

I, of course, have read several books about what to do. I have read Richard Ferber's classic, *Solve Your Child's Sleep Problems*, as well as *Sleeping Through the Night* by Jodi Mindell, who seems to be known in sleepless circles as the kinder, gentler Ferber. I have read The *No-Cry Sleep Solution* by Elizabeth Pantley and *Healthy Sleep Habits, Happy Child* by Marc Weissbluth. Basically, they all come down to the same conclusions: we can sleep with Hannah for the next few years, we can buck up and live with night-waking, or we can draw a line in the sheets. We are at the end of our respective ropes. We decide to Ferber her.

Richard Ferber (man, not verb) is the optimistic—some would say heartless—doctor who advocates letting your child cry for increasing increments of time in order to teach him or her how to fall asleep. I know it's supposed to work. I know research supports it. Several of our friends have used it and swear by it. I'm ready to try anything.

We choose a time to implement the good doctor's recommendations. Jane tells our friend Mark what we are going to do. Because he is either a saint or a masochist, he offers to come over. On Friday evening, we have dinner, then bathe Hannah and get her ready for bed, as though nothing untoward is about to happen. Jane feeds her. We read to her, as usual. *Big Red Barn, Good Night Gorilla, Jamberry*.

Then I walk Hannah back and forth for a couple of minutes in her room, singing to her as I do every other night. But instead of continuing until she is fast asleep, I put her in her crib and leave the room. She is horrified.

I go into the living room. Hannah bellows. The three of us sit and listen. Mark tries to distract us by talking about something else, but there is only one subject. Hannah yells. She rages. She screams. We have already decided, based on our halfhearted previous attempts to use the Ferber method, that we cannot go back into her room every few minutes the way that he suggests. Doing this only throws kerosene on her flames.

We have read that most children cry for no more than forty-five minutes or so. Ten minutes go by. Then fifteen. Then twenty. Then she vomits.

Jane and I go back in, as the book instructs, and quickly and more-or-less calmly change her sheets. Then we put her back in the crib and leave. Hannah is aghast.

Mark suggests that we all go downstairs to the basement. We have the baby monitor on, of course, although at Hannah's current volume, it is redundant. I tell them to go. In truth, I want them out of the room. I want to be alone, to stand like a barrier island absorbing the waves of Hannah's fury. I sit in the blue armchair in the living room, staring down the hallway toward Hannah's room while she screams. Thirty-five minutes go by, then forty-five, then fifty. There is no slowdown apparent. We hit an hour. Hannah keeps screaming. Then an hour and a half. Occasionally, she stops for a minute or two and my stomach begins to unfurl, but she always starts again. Two hours. Two and a quarter hours. Two and a half hours.

Finally, there is quiet. I wait. A minute goes by, then three, then five. I crane my head down the hall. I hear her breathing, but otherwise, only silence. I wait another five minutes, then slip into her room. Hannah is asleep, but slumped in a sitting position against the bars of her crib. She is hot and sweaty and wet from tears. I feel as though I have broken her spirit, as though I will find a docile, cowed child in her crib in the morning.

I lay her down, delicately, and pull a blanket up to her waist. She shudders, but does not wake. She sleeps.

Miraculously, she continues to sleep. She wakes around two o'clock, as usual, and I go into her room, check on her, and then leave. Jane and I lie in bed listening to her cry and watching the clock. Five minutes. Ten. Fifteen. And then quiet. I am stunned.

The next night, we do it again. Hannah wails for an hour and a half, but then falls asleep.

The following night, I am prepared for at least forty-five minutes of screaming. Instead, she cries a little, but falls asleep within ten minutes. Jane and I are speechless. I go to the door of Hannah's room and peer in to make sure she hasn't packed her bag and moved out. But she is still there, lying in her crib, asleep. Jane and I sit on the couch, flabbergasted. We can have a life, or at least an evening. I barely know what to think.

NINE

Flight

[1]

NEW YEAR'S DAY AND HANNAH IS TAKING OFF. Two weeks ago, at ten-and-a-half months, she started to pull herself up onto gelatin legs, tugging on the edges of chairs and tables. She has pulled a dining-room chair down on herself, resulting in a bump the size and color of a blackberry on the back of her head. The next day, she did it again. Today, I hold onto the chair and admire her persistence. The drunkenness of her gait is wearing off. She stands with increasing confidence. She grasps the table or the toy basket and, showoff that she is, waves the other hand in the air. She is an athlete triumphant. She is a victor. She is a queen.

She stands behind the plastic Push-N-Ride that I bought her for Christmas and tools around the basement. The yellow-and-red version, for boys, was labeled as suitable for children nine months and up. The exact same toy, in pink-and-blue for girls, was marked appropriate for children ten months and up. I went with the boy version because I like to think that she is precocious and also because of the nifty storage space behind the seat. Hannah grasps the back of the scooter and takes off, walking at a forty-five-degree angle when the cart gets out ahead of her. But she stays upright, like a sailboat tilting in the wind.

I am insanely proud of Hannah for walking. The problem is that she never wants to stop.

Within twenty-four hours of discovering the pleasures of the

Push-N-Ride, Hannah decided that sleep did nothing but interfere with walking. After a four-week reprieve of Ferber-induced sleep, Hannah is waking again, five, six, seven times a night. She stands at the end of her crib, wailing. She pulls her knees up under her stomach and lurches across the mattress. She rolls from side to side. We read in one of our many guidebooks to babies that major developmental milestones (like, say, walking) can "disrupt" sleep. This one has chewed up sleep and spit it into the gutter. "It's your fault, you know," Jane says to me. "You got her that damn scooter."

I feel like I'm living with a two-foot-tall, psychotic dictator. I lie in bed at night, undecided about whether to trust myself to sleep or whether it's wiser just to stay awake forever. I drift off. Sometimes, completely randomly, I am allowed to sleep. Other times, she begins to holler and I haul myself out of bed to the insistent drumbeat of Hannah's stomping, thumping, walking feet on the mattress of her crib.

[11]

What is the shape of parenthood? It is linear, building daily on itself. Experience grows with the child. Skills build sequentially, one mastery laying the foundation for the next. The child rolls over, sits up, stands, walks, runs. The child grows physically, mentally, emotionally. The parent learns to read emotions and cries, learns to store extra diapers in the glove compartment of the car, learns to scan each new environment for potential hazards. The child's body gains inches. The mind grows synapses. Hearts gain strength. Life is measured initially in weeks, then months, then years. Tripping and stumbling, reaching out for balance, parent and child go forward, marching into the future.

At the same time, parenthood is circular. The days cycle indistinguishably: wake, diaper change, play, eat, bottle, sleep, wake, diaper change, play, eat, bottle, sleep, wake, diaper change, play, eat, bottle, sleep. I often don't know what day it is; just that it is naptime or lunchtime or playtime.

Fears double back on us, sometimes morphing in form, sometimes just sneaking up from behind. The same problems surface and resurface, like recurring melodies.

"I'm really tired of having this discussion," Jane says to me one evening after asking me, again, if something is wrong and hearing, again, that everything is fine, just fine. "Do you even see it as a problem?"

There is a brick in my stomach, its sharp corners cutting my membranes. "Yes," I say because I feel like there is no other answer. I feel pressed into a corner. I want to evaporate.

"I feel like I have to fight your insecurities to get to you," she says. "I'm really sick of it. I don't have the energy for this."

What triggered this conversation, I barely remember. I'm not sure it matters. When I am upset about something (a failure, a fear, a preoccupation, a wound), I slip into distance. As though in my own private Narnia, I travel in another country.

Jane reminds me that we are not talking about an incident, we are talking about a pattern. I would rather talk about something specific, something literal, something I can get my hands around and explain or escape. A pattern feels hopeless to me. A pattern feels ingrained. It feels like personality.

"What do you suggest we do?" Jane asks. She looks worn. The muscles in her face are taut.

I suggest we run away. I suggest we prostrate ourselves and apologize for our failures and start being good. I suggest we reform. I suggest we dig our fingernails into our thighs. I don't say any of this.

"Um, well, exercise helps."

Jane looks at me.

"It helps when I can get time to write. I just need to do more of that. In the evenings, I guess."

"I think you've drawn even further into yourself since being at home with Hannah. I don't even know where you are."

I say nothing.

"Do we need to go talk to someone?" she asks. She means a therapist. Great, I think. We could sit on the couch in the therapist's office and discuss Me and My Issues. My Problems, without which everything would be fine.

I don't want to commit to anything. "Maybe. I don't know," I say.

What are we talking around?

[111]

Jane tells me that I always seem angry. My response, which I keep to myself, is Fuck You. This may be an indication that she is right. This makes me angry.

True to form, I don't know exactly what's going on. I know that my temper is dry like kindling. I know that Jane is driving me crazy. I know that I'm frustrated because I'm not writing with any consistency, which makes me feel lazy and constipated and sad. I tell myself that all of this is because I'm overcome by the Long Sleeplessness. And that it's hard to take care of a baby who insists on becoming a toddler.

I am angry because the house is a mess and I feel like I have failed in my housewifery. I feel guilty because Jane comes home from work tired and I'm tired and I want to go away and, instead, we give Hannah a bath because she's covered in food from dinner, and then it's time to make our dinner and do the dishes that have collected on the counter like ants around spilled ice cream. I feel guilty because I'm not earning money. I am angry because any writing I do for money takes away from the limited time I have to do any other writing. I am convinced that I will have to go back to a full-time fundraising job and I'll hate it. I feel a need to prove and prove and prove to Jane that taking care of Hannah is hard. I am sick and tired of picking up and picking up again the books and CDs that Hannah has pulled off our shelves and dumped onto the living-room floor. I hear Jane's voice as criticism, no matter what she says. She looks at me with worn-out frustration. I bite.

We sit in the basement after Hannah has gone to bed and watch television. I feel like our time together has dropped to this lowest common denominator: sitting in the same room. Sometimes the ice thaws. She relaxes into me and I into her, but it never seems to last.

Jane asks me what's wrong. "I'm fine," I say. It's a lie that I don't even try to make ring true. I'm not trying to cover my tracks. I just want to be left alone.

She asks again. I feel cornered. "I'm tired." This, at least, is true, but it's not the source of the problem.

We pick at each other.

[IV]

Mark, God bless him, has offered to babysit on Friday, the night before Valentine's Day, so that Jane and I can go out. We have decided to have a joint celebration of Valentine's Day and Jane's birthday, which was a week earlier. Jane wants to have sushi and a martini, the utterly off-limits fantasy meal that has sustained her throughout the food taboos of pregnancy and nursing.

I go to the store midweek to find a Valentine's Day card. I pass by the florid cards for "My Wife," although I am always a little tempted to get one of those, and the array of cards with cartoon drawings of little boys and girls or middle-aged boys and girls. Finally, I find one I like, two pen-drawn, nondescript animals holding a heart. I tuck the card away until a few hours before we are scheduled to go out.

Inside, the card says, "Be My Valentine." Simple, straightforward. I like that. The problem is that I have no idea what else to write. In years past, it has come easily to me, words of friendship and love grown deep into the soil of our lives. But now, I hold the pen and stare.

We have been bickering all day, again, and what I want more than anything right now is to go down to the basement with a book and my pillow. I want to stop being at the beck and call of the baby. I want to stop being annoyed by everything Jane does or doesn't do. I want to stop watching her set her jaw when I say something that irritates her or turn away when I say something that upsets her. I want to know what to do about this. I want to care enough to do it.

This doesn't seem like the right sentiment for a valentine.

I have to write something.

"Let's rediscover each other." It's the only thing that comes to mind. It rings vaguely of the excitement of our early friendship, when every conversation, every walk across campus, every class, every meal was a time to learn each other's landscape.

I seal the card and stick it in my purse.

Seated at the sushi bar, martinis in place, miso soup finished, and spicy tuna rolls on the way, I hand Jane the card. She reads it. "I think there's a theme here," she says. She gives me a card. "This has been such a hard year," she wrote, "full of more peaks and valleys than ever before in our relationship. I just want you to know that I'm committed to you. I want to rediscover all of the laughter and passion that made us fall in love with one another in the first place."

I feel as though I have caught a glimpse of something loved and lost. I feel enormously soothed that we have both written about rediscovery, as though, in our separation, we are still connected. I am pleased that Jane remembers what made us fall in love in the first place and that, on some level, she misses it. I feel my body relaxing. I slide my knee next to hers. I feel like a door is opening again, that I can return to a world too long closed off.

By Monday morning, we are back in our routine. We are both tired. Jane has to leave early to go to a meeting. She is in the dining room giving the baby her daily oatmeal while I take a shower. I lean my forehead against the tiled wall and let the water soak my hair. What is it that I'm trying to rediscover?

I want my Jane back. I want to reclaim the Jane I fell in love with. I want back the Jane who took care of me.

Can I rediscover her if I'm not sure she still exists?

I turn the water temperature up, to the heat of tears.

I miss what we used to be.

In no way, at all, ever, do I regret having a child. I knew that parenthood would change my relationship with Jane, but I did not know how fundamentally it would change. I did not know that our relationship would change so dramatically because we would change so radically.

Maybe rediscovery is the wrong word. Rediscovery may be linked too closely to reclaiming, reinhabiting, returning to something that was once known. It occurs to me that I cannot rediscover Jane because she is not who she used to be. Maybe what I need to do is discover who she is now, as a mother. Maybe we both need to discover who we are, together, as parents.

[V]

I feel like I am living in a house with a band of demented elves. Hannah is starting to run, apparently because she wasn't able to wreak enough destruction while walking. She pulls toys from her basket, looks at them, and tosses them over her shoulder onto the living-room floor. She surveys her work. She picks up her plastic soapdish and scoots over to the sofa, where she places it next to a pillow. She picks it up again and scoots under a table and into the corner behind a tall floor lamp. She peers over the arm of the sofa to make sure someone is watching and begins to swing the lamp. I tell her to come out from under the table. She grins. I reach for her. She pushes herself farther into the corner, slides down the wall, and sits on the floor gripping the lamp cord. Visions of electrocution flash through my mind. I pry her fingers loose and pull her out. She zooms into the kitchen, where she yanks open two drawers that Jane and I emptied permanently after all their contents were repeatedly hurled onto the floor. She puts the soapdish inside one drawer and closes it. Pulls it open. Still there. Shuts it. Pulls it open. Takes the soapdish out. She trots over to her cabinet full of Tupperware, opens the door, pulls out the shelf that is conveniently on wheels, sits down on the shelf, and begins strewing plastic items. She stands up and turns around. She spies a basket of bananas and pears and pulls it off the counter and onto the floor. She zips into the dining room. She pushes a chair into a corner. She whisks a napkin off the table. She stands back to get a better view of what else is up there. She spots the newspaper. She can't quite reach it, so she hangs on the edge of the table and wails. I give her a plastic block, which makes up for the withholding of the newspaper. She looks at it, deems it acceptable, and is off to the toy basket to start again.

[VI]

Finally, finally, the temperature has broken forty degrees, which feels luxuriantly summery after the months of ice and wind. I have packed Hannah into her backpack and taken her for a walk in a nearby park. She rides in her backpack like a horse, bouncing up and down and letting loose a whoop now and then. She has discovered, to her great delight, that she can lean forward and grab my hair, pulling on it like reins. She is my cargo; I am her steed.

Driving back from the park, with Hannah tucked into her car seat at a safe distance from my hair, I realize that I feel like a Mama. Jane asked me the other day, "Do you think of yourself as Hannah's mother?"

"No," I said, "I think of myself as her Mama." I am fluent in our one-way conversations. I am used to her feel, to her weight in my arms. I am used to the grip of her hand on my bicep. I've begun to readjust my expectations so that I am happy if we accomplish one thing in a day and positively giddy if we manage two. I have become used to a day that is defined by naptime and snacktime and lunchtime and second snacktime and dinnertime and bedtime. I know the halting whimpers that Hannah makes when she wants a bottle. I monitor the floor for chokeables—dried pieces of food, unidentified fallen objects, bits of leaves or gravel tracked in from outside. I know the sound of her breathing. I listen for her while I sleep.

In two weeks, Hannah will be one year old. She is oblivious to the milestone that keeps me sitting in the dark in her bedroom, listening to her breathe. It is irrelevant to her that I sat in that same spot one year ago wondering what she would look like and how she would feel in my arms. It makes sense to me now that so many books about parenthood cover the first year of the child's life. It takes that long to grow the heart and soul of a parent.

[VII]

Meanwhile, I continue to feel guilty for not earning money. I feel like I should protect Jane by taking care of everything around the house, but when I try to do so, I become resentful that I am taking care of everything around the house. I am annoyed with her for not picking up after herself, for leaving her pajamas balled up in the bathroom, for not hanging up the washcloth after she cleans Hannah's hands. I feel like I am following both of them around, cleaning up after them.

I need some time to myself, some time away from baby duty. But the truth is that I don't enjoy time away when I get it. I am at a loss, don't know what to do, end up going to a coffee shop and drinking cocoa and reading, feeling like I am not making good use of the time I have. Or I drive from place to place, undecided about what to do, finally deciding to run an errand. I feel frustrated. I feel defensive. I feel unproductive. I feel as though I have way too many feelings stuck inside my chest. I feel a little lonely.

Intellectually, I think that I don't need to feel guilty about not working, but I continue to do so anyway. I am unsure whether I can ever make decent money freelancing. I wonder if I will have to return to an office. I don't want to, which makes me feel guilty all over again. Jane gave me a calendar recently after returning from a brief business trip. She picked it up because she thought I would like the pictures. The voice in the back of my head pointed out that I could use it to mark the number of days until I have to return to work.

[VIII]

It strikes me as not a good thing that I often don't know if Jane and I are fighting. Tonight, after we eat dinner and after Hannah falls into sleep, Jane goes downstairs to watch TV. After a while, I follow her. She is lying on the couch, cat on her belly, another curled by her side. We talk for a moment, but she is tired. Ever since Hannah was born, Jane has gotten tired in a new way. She will seem fine, but then she will completely lose all energy, like air bursting out of a punctured balloon. She looks worn down, worn out, worn thin. She tells me that she isn't feeling well, that she doesn't know what's wrong.

All the energy that Jane and I used to pour into each other has been redirected by a pushy, eleven-month-old Corps of Engineers. When I am not with Hannah, I generally want to be alone. When Jane is not with Hannah, she generally wants to be asleep. Jane and I still spend time together, but it is bracketed by need. Dishes need to be done. Clothes need to be washed. The baby needs to be fed. Work needs to be tended. Someone, at some point, needs to sleep.

"Do you want me to leave you alone?" I ask. This is really a test question. If she is, in fact, sick, she will probably want me to stay. If she is upset, she will want me to go.

She nods.

I leave.

[IX]

Snow is predicted, but warmth is not far behind. This is early March in Minnesota: heavy dumps of snow followed by warm, mud-stirring air. Hannah has been napping for the past hour but has just begun to stir. I don't want her awake yet. It is too early; waking now will sap the rest of the day, like a February warm spell that spurs trees into budding too soon. I slip into her room and lift her out of the crib. I lower myself gently into the glider and hold her, her head resting in the bend of my elbow. My right arm supports her bottom. Her chest and stomach press against me. Her feet rest on the arm of the chair. Hannah twitches, whimpers, then tips back into sleep.

I gaze at her, trying to memorize exactly how she looks and how she feels. I try to catch and hold her soft breath, but it is as mild and fleeting as the scent of a crocus. I want to hold this moment, but I know it will escape me. Already, I look at the pictures of Hannah when she was newly home from the hospital or when she was just learning to bat at toys or just beginning to eat cereal. I barely remember her as she was. I recall her past like a film I saw once, long ago, that has become hazy with time. What she is now, in this moment, is everything. All her Hannahness fills this day.

[X]

Spring is letting loose in Minnesota. Today is far too gorgeous to stay inside, the grass greening, the sky blue. Jane has come home early from work, unable to sit any longer in her basement office. We put Hannah's pink suede shoes on her feet, double-knot the laces, and take her outside. She has been outside many times, of course, but this is the first time that she can actually walk around. During the winter, I pulled her in the snow on her sled, but she was so bundled in her pink snowsuit that she was nearly immune to the weather. She sat expressionless on the red plastic sled, arms sticking out at forty-five-degree angles, while a few snowflakes collected on her nose. But today it is warm and delicious and she is waking up to the world. She lurches through the grass like a foal new on its feet. She plops down to investigate leaves and twigs, to pull dead grass out of the ground and rub it in her hair. She flaps her arms with the excitement of it all.

Hannah feels her way through the yard. She finds a plant pot half-full of melted snow, dips her hands in, and comes out covered with grit. Hannah, with bits of leaves and woodchips stuck to her shirt and pants. Hannah, turning and looking in all directions, soaking in the grass and the trees and the birds and the sky. Hannah, learning to run. Hannah, flapping her arms. Hannah, my Hannah, I believe you can fly.

TEN

Shards

I FANTASIZE ABOUT SLEEPING through the night. Most nights, I tell Jane to go downstairs to the basement to sleep. I do this for several reasons. First, I see no sense in having both of us up whenever Hannah wakes. Second, I seem to have better luck getting Hannah back to sleep. Third, I feel guilty enough for not working and even more so if Jane is up at night. I tell Jane to go downstairs and she goes. What I want, secretly, is for her to argue, to tell me, no, no, you should sleep. But Jane does not have the energy to resist. So I walk Hannah back and forth and back and forth. I have done this enough that I can close my eyes while I walk, in imitation of sleep. I fantasize about a retreat center that I visited once, run by renegade nuns in the north woods of Minnesota. I imagine that I am there, alone, blessedly alone. I walk through the door of the private cabin, or "hermitage," set some books that I have brought along on the table, and lie down on the twin bed that is covered in a patchwork quilt. I imagine sleeping and waking at will. I imagine getting up whenever I feel like it, lying in bed reading, eating as slowly as I choose. Night after night, I visit.

At Hannah's naptime, I lie down on the sofa, like all the books advise, to get some rest. Just as I am drifting off, I hear a loud thump. I jolt awake. It could be Hannah careening out of her crib.

Or maybe something fell on her, a tree, perhaps, or a chunk of ceiling or a piece of sky. I go to check. Hannah is sleeping soundly. There is no sign of any disturbance in her room. I know that I heard something, but I have no way of knowing if it was real, or if it was like the phantom cries that I sometimes hear in the night, when I wake certain that Hannah is calling for me while, in fact, she is fast asleep.

Here is the truth: when Jane was pregnant, I found her irresistible. I loved her scent, her roundness, her exuberant possibility. I don't find postpartum Jane irresistible. I don't even find her attractive. I don't find myself attractive. I have no interest whatsoever in sex, other than in a purely theoretical way. I don't know why this is. I know that birth mothers often lose interest in sex for several months after birth, but I am not a birth mother. I can't blame this on hormones. I feel guilty for feeling this way. I am afraid that our relationship is withering. At the same time, I can't quite summon the energy or the interest to do anything about it.

Every now and again, we go out on a date. My sister or Mark comes to sit for Hannah, and Jane and I scoot away, clutching the cell phone and a few hours. We go to a restaurant or a movie. We take a walk around a lake. It is like looking through a window at a life we once lived.

I have come to believe that there are two things people consistently lie about: the condition of their house when they bought it ("it was *immaculate!*") and the ease with which their young child sleeps. For a long time, I felt a sense of curdling hostility toward anyone who claimed either of these almost unimaginable successes. I feel better now that I have decided that they are filthy liars. I consider telling everyone I meet that Hannah voluntarily climbs into bed, blows a kiss at us, and sleeps twelve uninterrupted hours every night.

The thought occurs to me, like a slight breeze through an open window, that I might not need to manage Jane. It occurs to me, too, that this is how I have always responded to stress or conflict or anger: to manage the things or the people around me. It also occurs to me that this drives Jane batty. I do it anyway.

Jane is back from a few days in Vancouver, where she attended a conference for work. I think I should be happy to have her back, excited to hear about her adventures, but truthfully, I am not. What I am is irritated.

Do we know each other anymore?

Jane tells me that she realized how alienated she has been feeling from herself—physically, emotionally, and psychically. She says that she doesn't know who she is—as a mom, a partner, or an employee. She says she feels perpetually inadequate and stressed out.

We scratch at each other. Jane complains that we always and only talk about tasks and schedules and ordering things. She suggests that we hire a housekeeper to come in every few weeks. I hear this as accusation: you are not holding up your end of the bargain.

. . .

Hannah catches a cold. And then Jane and I catch it. Jane has been coughing for weeks, a loud, wracking cough that makes the veins in her throat stand out. She has trouble sleeping because she is coughing. I send her downstairs, again, because her cough will wake the baby, wake me, wake the neighbors.

I pick another fight. I'm not sure why. I don't know if I need more time alone or more time together. I'm not sure if I need to get my shit together and get a job or if I need to be a better homemaker. I'm not sure if this is a symptom of sleep deprivation or a lack of exercise or a lack of compassion. I think surly thoughts about Jane. Except when we go out on a date, I am not attracted to her physically, which frightens me. I want to be close, but I no longer feel like I know how.

Jane says she wants time together, the two of us, to just "be." Good, fine, I think, but the closest we seem to come to that is watching television. We can just "be," but can we be together?

When I am stressed, I withdraw. I want to put things in order— emotions, rooms, Jane. When Jane is stressed, she resists order. She wants to sleep, to hibernate, to curl up with the cats.

Who is Jane as a mother? She is ferociously protective. She is anxious. She is loving and devoted, fun and funny. She is more emotionally vulnerable than I have ever seen her. She is proud. She is amazed. She is knowledgeable and nurturing. She is exhausted.

• • •

Years ago, I read a book about what makes long-term lesbian relationships work. Turns out it's not codependency, which strikes me
as hopeful news. After interviewing several couples, the authors
determined that the glue that keeps these relationships together
is really pretty simple: the women assume that they will stay together. They assume that they have a future. I think I still assume
the fact of our future, but it has grown murky. I don't want to
break up, but I also don't want to spend the next twenty years feeling disconnected from Jane. I don't want to assume the future of a
relationship that feels, at the moment, like it exists principally in
memory.

I go to a party hosted by friends from the church we used to attend. Hannah comes with me. Jane stays home to sleep. While
we are there, I meet a woman who is pregnant with her second
child. She tells me that she is nervous because having the first child
was so hard on her relationship with her husband. She tells me
that they went to therapy and that the therapist told them that it
takes about eighteen months to adjust to the addition of any new
child into the family. I'm not sure if I find this hopeful or depressing. We can make it to eighteen months, I think. But what will
happen then?

Jane and I swing from enraptured to exhausted, exhilarated to anxious. It is like our formerly stable relationship has suddenly gone
bipolar. I want more time with Jane, but I also want more time
alone. I want time alone, but I immediately miss Hannah. Then,
when Jane and I finally have some time together, what do we do?
We talk about Hannah.

• • •

What has happened to us, besides the obvious? I like to think that I was not hopelessly naive. I expected a period of adjustment after crossing the line into parenthood. I expected change. I expected a steep learning curve. I knew that we would be anxious and tired and emotional. But I did not expect that parenthood would rattle the bones of life as we knew it.

ELEVEN

For Better or For Worse

[I]

IT'S THE DAY BEFORE EASTER. I want to be thinking about egg hunts and instead, I've got vomit on my hands. Hannah is throwing up all over the living room. She has been logy for the past few days, with diarrhea showing up in her diapers. This morning, she was running a low temperature. Then in the early afternoon, she started to puke. Jane called the nurse. Give her fluids in small but steady amounts, the nurse advised. Pedialyte is good, she said. I went to Walgreen's to get a jug of Pedialyte for Hannah and three bags of Ricola cough drops for the wracking cough I developed sometime last week. Hannah has no interest in Pedialyte, although the wrappers from the cough drops are mildly intriguing to her. She vomits again.

Jane calls the clinic and makes an appointment to see a doctor. We are assigned to someone who is not our regular physician. We pack Hannah into the car, Jane sitting by her side in the backseat. I drive to the clinic. Hannah's stomach seems to have quieted. We are taken to an exam room where we recite Hannah's litany of symptoms for the nurse, who diligently writes everything down in her folder. We repeat the symptoms for the doctor, a large, friendly-looking man, when he comes into the room. "Sounds like a stomach bug," he says. "We're seeing a lot of that right now." He looks at her, checking her eyes and mouth. "She's a little dehydrated," he says. "That's not surprising. But she's mild." The main thing, he tells us, is to keep Hannah hydrated. "Keep giving her fluids, a little at a time. Just a swallow every few minutes." She'll be fine, he assures us. Just go on home and push the fluids. This will run its course.

So we go. On the way home, Hannah vomits again. We get home and I settle down on the couch with a plastic syringe that we have used to give Hannah medicine in the past. I suck Pedialyte into it from a glass and squirt some into the corner of Hannah's mouth. She takes it and seems to feel a little better. A few minutes later, Hannah takes a little more. Again, a few minutes pass. I try again. This time, Hannah flails her head around, her lips welded shut. I attempt to sneak the tip of the syringe past her defenses and squeeze the liquid into her mouth. She refuses and the orange fluid runs down her chin and into the folds of her neck. She wails. I rock her and talk to her. After a few more minutes, I suck some more Pedialyte into the syringe. I soothe her as I bring the tip to her mouth. She howls and wags her head. I stop. Over the next hour, I get a few more squirts in her mouth. Hannah calms momentarily each time but then revs back up. Nonetheless, I feel as though I have accomplished something. I report proudly to Jane that Hannah has taken a few ounces of fluid. Then she vomits.

Jane calls the nurse again. She tells her what has happened and what the doctor said. The nurse begins to recommend small amounts of fluid and large amounts of patience. Then she hears Hannah wailing in the background.

"Is that your daughter?" she asks. No, it's a CD of a wailing baby that we play for fun.

"Yes," Jane replies.

"She sounds pretty miserable," the nurse says. "You might want to take her to Children's."

Jane gets off the phone. "We're going to the hospital," she says.

When Hannah is not screeching, she lies limp in my arms. Jane gets her purse and I get a couple of towels to wipe up the vomit that I'm sure is still coming. We get into the car. I don't have the heart to snap Hannah into her car seat, and anyway, I am afraid that she will vomit and choke. I sit in the back seat holding Hannah on my lap while Jane drives. She blows through red lights. When we get there, Jane pulls up in front of the entrance to the emergency room. I ask Jane to take Hannah inside because she is the medically knowledgeable one in our family. I generally like a doctor if he or she seems nurturing. Jane actually knows something and can evaluate diagnoses and ask intelligent questions about treatments and differentials. Jane lifts Hannah from my arms and goes inside.

She tells me later that the nurse in the emergency waiting room took one look at Hannah and realized that she was considerably more than mildly dehydrated. Seeing Hannah, limp and lying in Jane's arms, the nurse tested her blood sugar with a finger prick. It was much too low. By the time I get to the waiting room after parking the car, Jane and Hannah are already in an exam room. Hannah has thrown up again. Jane is holding an emesis bowl, which is just about the only thing that hasn't yet gotten vomit on it.

When Hannah is sick, I look to Jane as my barometer of urgency. It's a double-edged sword. She knows a lot about illness, but also a lot about the many things that can go wrong, the ways that hospitals fall down on patient safety, the things that can knock a patient over. What I want, to be honest, is for Jane to provide informed reassurance. But when Hannah is sick, our still mostly preverbal, slack-from-vomiting Hannah, Jane's anxiety spikes. She is afraid.

We wait in the emergency exam room. Bright pictures of polar bears are painted on the walls. A nurse comes in and tells us that they will try right away to get a line into Hannah. She sets up the necessary equipment: an IV bag and stand, some gauze pads, a needle. Another nurse comes into the room and begins to prep

Hannah's arm for the IV. She attempts to insert the needle. After a couple of unsuccessful tries, she goes to find yet another nurse. This third nurse is a tall, down-to-business woman who seems completely at ease with the task of sticking needles into tiny veins. The problem is that Hannah's veins don't want the needle. She tries Hannah's arms and hands, but it doesn't take. "It's because she's dehydrated," she says. "Her veins are collapsing." Hannah is rigid with rage. She screams, her face going from red to purple. "We'll keep trying," the nurse says calmly. Jane sits on a plastic chair next to me, her body taut and tightening every time the needle enters Hannah's limbs. Finally, the nurse tries a foot. She manages to squeeze the needle in and get the vein to accept the intravenous fluid. "We're in," she says.

Hannah lies on her back, exhausted. The fluid flows into her vein. She relaxes. Her body soaks up the sugary water like a dry sponge. Jane and I watch over Hannah, guarding her. An hour goes by. A doctor comes in to check on us. He is fairly young, handsome, and surprisingly snappily dressed for an emergency room physician. He checks over Hannah, who is lying quietly on the exam table. "She was pretty dehydrated," he says. "We're seeing a lot of this right now." He asks us various questions about her health, listens to her heart, looks at her eyes and mouth. "You're well cared for," he says quietly to Hannah. "You're lucky."

He leaves and another hour goes by. A nurse comes in to check on the progress of the IV. It is dripping along, watering Hannah. "We'll want to keep her overnight," she tells us, "to make sure that she gets enough fluid. We'll get you into a room in a little while."

We wait. Another hour goes by. Jane goes out to the nurses' station to check on what's happening. Nothing is happening. The room isn't ready for us yet, she is told. We wait.

Another hour goes by. And another. And another. Hannah sleeps on the exam table. Jane and I watch the television that is suspended from the ceiling. I eat cough drops. Jane gets two glasses of water and some cookies from a vending machine.

Around 2:00 a.m., we are told that there is a room for us upstairs. A nurse pushes Hannah's bed out of the emergency room. We pick up our towels and purses and cough drops and Kleenex and follow.

We are taken to what is apparently the infectious disease ward. Outside the door of each room is a sign instructing medical staff to wear masks and gloves when entering. The nurse pulls on a mask and opens the door. Inside, there is another family, watching a Disney video on the television. The nurse places Hannah onto the hospital bed and adjusts the metal railings. She points us to a chair that folds out into a cot. She suggests that we use the bathroom down the hall to minimize cross-infection with the other family. I think it's way too late for that.

The other little girl is crying. Hannah starts crying. The other little girl settles down for a while. Hannah settles down for a while. Then the tag-team wailing begins again. Meanwhile, Donald Duck squawks into the darkness. I lie on the cot, trying not to hack up a lung. If Hannah weren't attached to a bag of saline, I would just pick her up and leave. Jane tries to calm Hannah. Then Jane starts to get nauseous, whether from our shared virus or stress or both. She leaves the room, walks down the hall to the bathroom, and retches into the toilet. I get up and hold Hannah, standing next to her IV stand. When Jane returns, we wheel the stand over to a chair and I hold her and rock her. She snuffles and cries. I snuffle and cough. Jane goes down the hall again to vomit. This sucks.

On one of her trips to the bathroom, Jane spies an empty room. She comes back and tells me of her find. "God, get it," I say. She goes out to the nurses' station and cajoles a nurse into letting us move into the other room. Meanwhile, both girls are wailing. It's 3:30 a.m.

The new room is nirvana. It is quiet. It is calm. We can fill it with our own private germs. We can contaminate our own bathroom. We have a cot. We have a chair. Hannah can sleep. I sit in the armchair and cradle Hannah, IV tucked into her foot, her hand twirling my hair. She falls asleep.

Jane feels dreadful. She lies on the cot and tries to sleep. I have no intention of sleeping. I only want to hold Hannah, to keep vigil at her side as the long drink drips into her veins. The hours pass. Nurses check on us from time to time, monitoring the IV bag and dispensing Tylenol. In the morning, a resident with tousled hair checks on us, asking a series of questions about Hannah's condition. Jane misses his visit, since she is again in the bathroom, throwing up. I wait for him to recommend small sips of Pedialyte, but he doesn't.

By early afternoon, Jane and I are haggard. Hannah, on the other hand, is feeling pretty darn good. She has rounded out again, like a wilted plant that has come back to life after a slow and steady rain. One of the nurses who has been checking on Hannah during our stay comes into the room. I don't know for sure that she is a lesbian, but whatever gaydar I still have in my exhausted state tells me that she very well might be. That and the comments she keeps making about women's basketball. She has paid special attention to Hannah, checking on her often and telling her approvingly what a strong little girl she is.

The nurse tells us that her shift is over and offers to hold Hannah for a while so we can rest. I am so relieved, I could cry. I hand Hannah to her, and Jane and I lie down together on the cot. I feel absolutely safe with this nurse in the room. I don't think twice about lying down with Jane in front of her. I don't know if the nurse has children of her own, nor for sure that she is a lesbian. But what I understand to be true is this: that there are times, and I believe this to be one of them, when gay people open their arms wide to our children, when they see the children of two moms or two dads as belonging to the whole community. I have seen this before, when gay men or lesbians step in, usually informally and unofficially, and surround one child or another with an extra circle of protection and friendship and support. I don't know if this is exactly what is happening here, in this moment, and I am far too tired to try to figure it out. I lie on the cot next to Jane. Before I close my eyes, I see our nurse sitting in the armchair, cuddling Hannah in her arms.

[11]

On the last Sunday in June, we pack the stroller, some sippy cups, a bag of snacks, hand wipes, diaper wipes, diapers, a change of clothes, sunscreen, Hannah's floppy sun hat, and various other things that we can't possibly survive half a day without. And we're off, like a couple of maternal pack mules with their young, to the Gay Pride parade. We drive to downtown Minneapolis, park the car, and walk along the parade route until we find a clearing big enough for the three of us and our cargo, about two-thirds of the way through the route. This way, we figure, we can watch for a while and then join the parade. We claim our patch of pavement, planting the stroller squarely in the middle of it.

Gay Pride in the Twin Cities is a serious thing. In addition to the parade through downtown, there is a two-day festival in nearby Loring Park, with rings of exhibitor tents circling the small lake. Corporations hand out pens and candy and plastic mugs, all helpfully imprinted with their name and logo. Realtors angle for new customers, churches for congregants, politicians for votes. Artists sell pottery and rainbow wind socks. Some lesbian invariably sells crafty trinkets decorated with pictures of cats. Between the festival and the parade, some four hundred thousand people turn out, making ours the third largest Gay Pride event in the nation.

Jane and I stand on the sidewalk, reapplying sunscreen to ourselves and to Hannah's pudgy legs and arms, despite the delightfully cool weather. Finally, the parade begins and, oh God, we forgot that it is led every year by Dykes on Bikes. Hannah begins to wail. It's not the dykes that are the problem; it's the bikes. The women inch by on their motorcycles, some circling, turning loops in the street, and driving by again. They rev their motors, the volume soaring. Naturally, it's a huge contingent. Every dyke with a bike between here and Fargo has apparently shown up this year. The noise builds all around us. I feel like I have a lawnmower in my head. I hold Hannah and scoot back against the wall of the building behind us, telling her they will be gone soon. She buries her teary face in my shoulder, her hands pressed against her ears.

Once the motorcycles have passed, the parade is fun again for Hannah. We wave at the "princesses" in their elaborate gowns, their titles—like Miss Gay Southeast Minnesota—proudly displayed on their pageant sashes. We watch the gay marching band. We cheer for the gay and lesbian teachers and flight attendants. We wave at the teenagers from District 202, a community center for queer youth.

Eventually, we see the contingent from Rainbow Families, the local organization for lesbian, gay, bisexual, and transgender parents and parent wannabes. These are our people, the ones dressed in practical clothes with pockets full of Kleenex and individually wrapped hand wipes (OK, maybe that's just us), pushing strollers loaded with babies and supplies. Dads carry toddlers on their shoulders. Moms pull decorated wagons stuffed with kids and coolers stuffed with healthy sandwiches and juice boxes. Older children wave rainbow flags and scout the edges of the street for unclaimed candy thrown from the earlier floats.

"Here we go, Hannah," I say, as Jane pushes the stroller into the street. I have participated in a lot of Gay Pride parades in Minnesota, as well as in New York and occasionally Washington. But every time, I experience a rush. There is something exhilarating and wholly affirming about being part of this. The people lined along the sidewalk cheer as we walk by with the other families, just as they have for all of the other contingents, but I feel as though they are cheering just for us. I want to breathe this in, to hold on to the waves of applause.

It's not that I feel particularly oppressed, or even disapproved of, the rest of the year. Our families are supportive; our neighbors seem fine with the fact that Hannah has two moms. But at the same time, I always feel a difference between our family and straight families, one of nuance more than category. Our daily life is much like that of any family with a young child, but I can never wholly escape the sense that there is a kind of scrim between us. Sometimes, it manifests as a sense of vulnerability; more often, for me anyway, it's a vague but persistent sense of separateness. But here, surrounded by gay and lesbian and bisexual and transgender families, that sense of separation evaporates.

By no means are all these families just like ours; there is considerably more diversity among the families in our community than is generally recognized. Some have one parent, others two or more. Some are multiracial or have special-needs kids. Some have transgender parents. Others have adopted older children or are foster parents. But in this moment, our families can just be celebrated—without need for explanation or justification. And that's what is so powerful. It's not that our families are "just like" straight families; we're not, although our daily lives may be. It's not even that I want to be just the same. There are ways in which our family is different and will always be so. We are two lesbians who chose to have a baby; not two parents who just "happen" to be lesbian, in the same way that we happen to have brown hair. But here, there are no questions about what our families are like, or what it means to be a second mom or second dad, or how our children will fare. Here, we are just who we are.

At the end of the parade route, we funnel into Loring Park. The parents of young children head toward shady spots on the grass and begin spreading out blankets, laying out snacks, and changing diapers. The ones with older kids move toward the line of Port-o-Johns, the corn dog vendors and the playground. We decide to do the circuit of exhibitors, partly because it is our annual ritual and partly because I want to show Hannah off. We move from table to table, stopping along the way to chat with friends and casually positioning Hannah for admiration. Meanwhile, Hannah hauls. It turns out she's a gift magnet; she collects, among other things, two balloons, several fake tattoos, a jumble of Mardi Gras beads in rainbow colors, and a stuffed version of Target's Jack Russell mascot.

After an hour or so of this, Hannah is winding down and the stroller is getting full. We walk out of the park, leaving behind the rainbow flags and the music, the lip-syncing drag queens, the gay bankers and stilt walkers and community organizers, the clergy in their rainbow stoles and the couples preparing for the group commitment ceremony to be held later in the afternoon. Hannah is drifting to sleep, Mardi Gras beads clutched in her hand. The music follows us as we walk, lingering in the air as we make our way down the street, toward our car, toward home.

[111]

We get a call from the child care center at the university. They will have a place for Hannah in mid-July. A full-time place.

For some time now, we have been looking at various options for child care. Several months ago, Hannah and I visited one site that is part of a local, Montessori-based day care chain. It was nice enough; the front door opened into a common room that was bright and spacious. An aquarium bubbled against the wall. Windows looked into classrooms where three- and four-year-olds were busily working at two-foot-high tables.

Shirley was the director. She shook my hand and told me that she would lead us on the tour. I explained that we were interested in placing Hannah when she reaches sixteen months old—the official start of toddlerdom—so we went directly into the young toddler room. Two-year-olds and almost-two-year-olds clustered in a circle around Teacher Eileen, an attractive twentysomething woman who was gathering them for music time. She handed out small shakers and tambourines. Teacher Eileen led the children in singing the "Wheels on the Bus" song. A couple of stray toddlers roamed the room, one scratching his belly. A little girl lurched over to the director and looked up at Hannah. Shirley picked her up and asked if she wanted to say hello to the baby. "No," she chirped and squirmed to get down.

"We're licensed for twenty-one kids in here," Shirley told me, which struck me as barbaric. I am overcome by one child. Nonetheless, I couldn't help noticing that Teacher Eileen was managing to hold the attention of almost all of them. "The mommies on the bus say 'shh, shh, shh'" she sang. The children bounced along all over town.

We visited the older toddlers next. They were grouped around small tables. Some worked with clay. Some stacked blocks. Some were doing something or other with yarn. One child stood on the other side of the room, watching himself in front of a full-length mirror that said in block letters across the top, "YOU ARE SPECIAL."

Back in the common room, before we visited the next group, we walked past a dance class. A teacher led the kids through basic ballet steps. Their chubby four-year-old legs bent into crooked pliés. The girls were dressed in pink leotards, some with little tutus. In fact, everyone in the group was in a pink leotard. "Is this class just for girls?" I asked. "No," Shirley responded. "But only girls signed up. I don't know why. We had one little boy, but he didn't last."

"How do you teach the kids about diversity?" I asked at the end of the tour. Shirley paused for a minute, looking a little confused. "I mean, do you have some kind of curriculum that talks about different kinds of families?" She didn't answer. I took the plunge. "Hannah has two mommies. Do you talk with the kids about how people come from all different kinds of families?"

"Well," she said, "I guess we would answer questions if they came up."

To my ears, this had faint echoes of Don't Ask, Don't Tell. The reality is that children learn what is true and possible in the world based on what they see and hear around them. They play house and family. They talk about their mommies and their daddies. They read storybooks about traditional families. We have friends whose four-year-old daughter regularly comes home from day care and wants to play house, insisting that her Mommy be the mother and her Mama the father. I don't plan to sequester Hannah on Planet Lesbian, but I would like her to think, for as long as possible, that the composition of her family is just one of a multitude of options. I would like her to live in a world where some kids have two moms, some have two dads, some have grandparents, some have lots of siblings, some have one parent, some have stepparents. And, oh yeah, some boys dance.

I am disheartened, but the truth is that this day care center was really just a backup plan all along. When Jane was in her fourth month of pregnancy, she added her name to the waiting list for the university's child care program. Jane and I have both toured the center, with its bright "bungalows" awash in toys. We like the fact that the center not only thinks about diversity but is practically obsessed with it. The information they provide to us emphasizes the program's "non-bias" and nonviolent curriculum. The classrooms are decorated with tschotskes from all over the world: little dolls from Korea, a mobile from France, some leis from Hawaii, a rainbow flag. It's the flag that clinches it for us. We both feel that this is a place where our family will be neither frowned upon nor overlooked.

We regularly get mailings from the university's child care center asking us to update our contact information and suggesting, rather rigidly, I think, that if we fail to return the form in a timely fashion, we will be *dropped to the bottom of the list*. We have heard too many stories from other employees and students at the university about how they had to wait two or three years for a spot. After staying carefully in line as long as we have, we have no intention of being booted to the back. We fill out the forms right away, seal and stamp them, and make sure to get them into the mailbox.

Meanwhile, I have become consumed with the idea that something will happen so that we will never get in. Our paperwork will be lost in the mail, I think. The other toddlers will somehow all flunk toddlerhood and a space will never open up. I consider the possibility that I might continue to keep Hannah at home with me. On the one side, this sounds appealing. Then again, I think I might lose my mind.

What I really want is part-time day care for Hannah. It sounds like an enormous relief. I could do grownup things. I could do some work. I could answer the phone without fear. I could go out somewhere without hauling along diapers, wipes, and a bottle. I could recklessly stay out *past naptime*. But full-time day care just makes me sad. It makes me feel like I would never see Hannah, that my favorite playmate would be gone. I worry that Jane and I would wrestle for Hannah on evenings and weekends, because that's the only time we'd be with her. Meanwhile, someone else would watch her grow.

The practical side of my brain says that we should take full-time care and I should get a full-time job because I need to contribute to a 401K and bring money into the checking account and save money for college. But that is not what I want to do.

"Do you want me to get a job?" I ask Jane, innocuously, I think. We are sitting in the basement, the television muted, bowls just emptied of apple crisp on the end table. "Not necessarily," she says. "But I am concerned about our finances."

This is what I hear: Go get a job, loser. You are draining our bank account. You can stay with the baby until she's a toddler, but then you need to get a grip, buck up, shoulder your responsibility, earn some money.

"I feel a lot of pressure having the only full-time salary," she says.

And I think, what will I do? I don't want to get another fundraising job, but I don't know what my other options are.

We accept the full-time opening because not to do so would mean being *dropped to the bottom of the list*. I go with Hannah to the child care center on her first full day and stay so long that the teachers eventually throw me out. I drive one block away, then park the car and sit in the seat and cry. My little girl. I want her in the car seat behind me, jabbering away. I drive toward home, sobbing. But at the same time, I feel the tiniest inkling of relief.

We have told the enrollment coordinator at the center that we want to be on the list for a part-time position. One might open up within the next three months, she tells us. After five weeks, it does, but I have had a taste of my old life. During those weeks, I never exactly send Hannah to the center full-time; I keep her home one day a week or take her in late and pick her up early. Part of this is because I miss her, deeply, viscerally. Part of it, also, is because she is exhausted by the massive change in her life. When she stays home, we have Mama Days. We go to the park or maybe to the zoo. We run errands. We play. I love having her with me. I press my face against her hair and breathe in her scent, attempting to burn her essence into my memory. I do not want to let her go. But when she is gone, I am disturbingly elated to have my own time. I clean the house with abandon, no sixteen-month-old hollering that the vacuum is hurting her ears. I write. I take on freelance work. I sit down when I want to, get up when I want to, go outside when I want to, eat when I want to. I feel guilty for liking it, but I also feel as though I have been infused with my own self again.

[IV]

There's just this one thing. In the course of all our illnesses and developmental milestones and changes, I have somehow managed to become Hannah's transitional object. I am now the only one who can put her to bed, the only one who can possibly walk with her into sleep. Bedtime is becoming even more complicated as Hannah becomes more willful. Where Jane or I used to get away with a couple of stories and a couple of songs, I am now called upon to add multiple sips of water, walks around the room to the computer-chipped accompaniment of her Mozart Cube, and a medley of hymns. Now we're not just doing "Love Will Guide Us" but also "Silent Night," "Surely the Presence of Our God Is in This Place," "Away in a Manger," and "What Child Is This?" When I'm really desperate, I sing the "Alphabet Song," slowly and methodically, like a lullaby. Hannah wants to fall not only asleep, but deeply, snoringly asleep, while pressed against my body. Then, when she wakes at eleven thirty or twelve o'clock or, if I'm wildly lucky, one o'clock, she wants to come into the big bed and lie pressed against or sprawled on top of me.

Hannah is moss to my bark, white to my rice, barnacle to my hull. I am her chosen one, her security blanket. To be more precise, my hair is her security blanket. She has never become devoted to a favorite toy, a sock monkey, say, or a stuffed kitty. She has never had a favorite "lovey," like other children we know, who must sleep with their worn-thin blankie or hug Mr. Rabbit every night. But she has my hair. When I hold her, her hand moves immediately to my hair. Her fingers twirl strands of hair around them, tightly spiraling and then pulling taut. She grabs a fistful and holds on. She plucks at strands as though they are strings on a guitar. Her hand is a squirrel paw, scritching at my scalp. When she starts to drop into sleep, her arm sagging, I wait, counting slowly to ten. She begins to breathe heavily and deeply. I pull my head away, feeling the hair dislodge from her grasp, but then she jolts. Her hand shoots up and begins feeling frantically for hair. I consider shaving my head and weaving my hair into a wig for the one stuffed animal she seems to like, a squishy pink pig. I might be bald, but at least I could sleep.

TWELVE

Anniversary

MEN APPARENTLY HAVE TROUBLE remembering anniversaries. Lesbians celebrate them several times a year. Jane and I have the anniversary of our first kiss, which has now been usurped by Hannah's birthday. We have the anniversary of when we first met in September 1984. And we have the anniversary of our commitment ceremony, which we held more or less ten years after we met. Counting as liberally as possible, which I like to do because it is the most impressive, this September marks our twentieth year together.

After lengthy and soul-searching discussion, Jane and I make plans to go to a hotel for a night. This feels as earthshaking as the very first time we left Hannah with someone else while we made a hurried trip to Target. This time, we will leave for an entire evening, night, and morning, returning home in the early afternoon. My sister and her boyfriend have agreed to move into our house for the night and shepherd Hannah. I am willing to go to a hotel in downtown Minneapolis, but no farther. I know that we can get home in fifteen minutes if we need to. St. Paul is totally out of the question; that would be half an hour away.

Finally, I make a reservation at a downtown hotel. I am both nervous and giddy, like I am going on a first date, which, in a way, is what it is.

And then we get sick. This time, all three of us are hit simultaneously, our noses running, our phlegm dripping. I cancel the reservation and call Stace to let her know. "I'm still willing to do it another time," she says. "You guys need this."

We do need it. For the past year, I feel like I have been seeing Jane through the reverse end of a telescope. The harder I look, the more distant and remote our relationship seems. At least, this is true of the relationship I remember, the one that pulled me into its vortex of talk and dreams. I feel as though our relationship has spun off its axis, slipped out of orbit. Jane and I have become focused on Hannah, which is understandable and good, but in the course of things, we have forgotten to focus on each other.

And in the midst of all of this, everything changed. Jane has changed. I have changed. God knows our sleep patterns have changed. Our relationship has changed, so profoundly that I no longer know if I recognize it. Where I used to be so certain that I stood on solid ground, I now feel the earth move beneath my feet. I am not sure I know anymore who we are, together or apart.

Is this just the way of things? Is it just what happens after twenty years plus one kid? Are we simply experiencing what every couple experiences in the post-post-post-honeymoon years?

This is not at all the way I imagined things would be. Twenty years ago, Jane was new to me. I was absorbed by her, overcome by her. Twenty years ago, we lay on the couch in the lounge of our dorm and talked about the books we were reading. We went to the ice cream shop and strolled across our achingly green central Indiana campus, eating butterscotch-twirl ice cream cones. We got drunk on Little Kings Ale with Deluxe Graham chasers. I laughed hysterically at her impression of a deer and teased her about her habit of talking to nuthatches and chickadees. We made up businesses we would launch, trips we would take, books we would write. We were blissfully fused and merged and all the things that lesbian couples supposedly are. We were in love.

Ten years ago, we had left Indiana and then New York for Minnesota. We gathered our friends and stood in front of an altar that was draped with a rainbow flag. We promised to love each other, to cherish each other, to laugh with each other, to talk with each other, to never leave.

Then, Jane was radiant to me. I basked in her. Then, we orbited each other. And now?

Today, we live in a suburban rambler built in 1955, the apex of American squareness. We have a child. We drive a station wagon. Our attention is sucked up by developmental milestones and diapers and formula. Our energy is drained by night wakings and recurring colds and our personal rosters of anxiety. We spend our evenings feeding Hannah, bathing Hannah, dispensing bottles, and reading *Big Red Barn*. There are always dishes on the counter and bits of hardened food on the floor. We are tired. No, we are sapped. In the evenings, we watch TV. Or we just go to bed. Most of our outings are to Target or the grocery store.

On the night we were supposed to go to the hotel, we are home instead. I make a turkey meatloaf, glazed with ketchup, and a pot of mashed potatoes. Jane goes downstairs to get a bottle of wine. I sit on the enclosed porch while Hannah, oozing snot, pushes her yellow and red racer across the floor in front of me. *A Prairie Home Companion* plays on the radio. Jane and I have been listening to this show, on and off, for the entire time we have been together. I look out the windows at our neglected gardens, with their overgrown lilies and overenthusiastic weeds. The sky is blue, the air is cool. It is a September evening in Minnesota.

I hold the card I bought for Jane. It has a drawing of a tugboat on the front, sailing on the open sea. "My little ship came in," it says, "and you were on it." Inside, it just says, "Lucky, lucky me," which I do realize could be interpreted in multiple ways. There are no florid sentiments. There are no flowers, no rainbows, no promises or declarations. There are not even any people. I like its simplicity. I think I like its open-endedness.

For years, I have given Jane anniversary cards in which I have written a portion of the vows I made to her when we had our commitment ceremony ten years ago: "I chose you long ago, and I choose you now." Today, I don't do that. I hold the card. I hold the pen. I wait.

Hannah comes over to peer at what I am doing. So far, I'm not doing anything. I wipe Hannah's nose with a Kleenex from the box that I am considering Velcroing to my thigh. I smell meatloaf in the oven. I listen to the music on the radio. I listen to Jane cough as she walks back upstairs. I think about what I could say about the last twenty years and, even more so, what I could possibly say about the past year. I look at the lingering flowers in our garden and the lowering rays of the early fall sun.

And this is it, isn't it? This is where we are, the three of us, in our garden of flowers and weeds. This is where we are, with our snot and our sunshine. This is where we are, even if, after a year and a half, it still sometimes feels off-balance and unfamiliar.

I begin to write: "Dear Jane. I don't mind that we didn't go to the hotel because I am happy to spend time here with you and Hannah. This and meatloaf and good wine and tickling and nice music—this is what our twenty years are all about."

It's not poetic. It's not profound. It's not romantic. But in this moment, at least, it seems to make sense to me. And in this moment, at least, it is true. I don't know where our relationship is going, although I am beginning to recognize that the one direction it is not going is back to what it used to be. I don't know exactly what it will mean to discover, or rediscover, Jane. I don't know what it will mean for her to discover, or rediscover, me. I don't know what we will find, or what we will find missing. I am beginning to understand how parenthood has changed us over the past year and a half, but I have no idea what it will do to us next year or the year after that. I don't know when I will ever get some reliable sleep. I don't know if Jane and I will ever again have the kind of intensive time for each other that we had before we became parents. I don't know what we would do with it if we did.

But I do know a few things. I know that Hannah is my beloved girl. I know that Jane and I struggle, and our relationship has changed profoundly, but it is still here. We are still here and we are still together. I am no more in love with change than I ever was before, but I know that, mostly, I would not alter the circumstances that have brought us to this place. I know with complete conviction that I would never, ever change having Hannah. I still wonder who I am as a parent, but I know that I am someone different than I was before. I know that Jane is Hannah's mother and I am Hannah's mama. I know that Jane is passionately in love with Hannah. I know that this is something vital, something urgent, something essential that we share.

And I know that we are still finding our way. We just might get there. Wherever there is.

I close the card, put it in the envelope, and prop it next to Jane's plate. I herd Hannah toward her high chair. It's time to sit down at the table. It's time to eat.

Epilogue

TIME PASSES; sometimes faster. Hannah is six now and in kindergarten, some days still a little girl, other days almost a pre-teen. I look at the framed series of ten photos that I took when she was a baby. "Five Minutes in the Life of Hannah," I call it, captured when she was four days old. She squints. She frowns. She purses her lips, closes her eyes, opens her eyes, sleeps. I remember those days—the wonder and panic and numbing exhaustion—but at the same time, I don't remember. What matters is Hannah now. She is strong and loud and emphatically independent. She overflows with laughter and sloppy kisses. She bursts with frustration. She inhales stories like air. She is clear that she wants to be famous one day, and stands in front of her full-length mirror practicing her rock-star moves. She is mine, she is ours, she is her own self.

To each other, we have grown into our own way of being family. Jane is the Primary Breadwinner, but also the cozier snuggler, the softer touch, the one who never tires of playing Barbie. I am usually at home, so I am generally the one who sits with Hannah during sickness, the one who takes her to school, the one who makes annoying rules about how much television is too much. But I am also the one who wrestles with her on the living-room floor, the one who cuddles her at bedtime, and the one who is always ready to go get ice cream.

Now that Jane is no longer pregnant or nursing, it is less apparent to the rest of the world which one of us is the biological mother and which one of us is not. Some of the legal vulnerabilities remain, but we have encased ourselves, as well as we can, in protective legal documents. I sometimes wonder how relevant it is anymore that I am Hannah's nonbiological mother. I'm not sure that it makes any appreciable difference in our daily life, but still, it does matter, at least to me. I am not a paternal stand-in, not an extension or replication of Jane. I am Hannah's Mama, and that is something different from the other categories, something that is distinct from mother and father, something that is new in the world.

Six years with Hannah, nearly twenty-five with Jane, and where are we? The fact that we are still together is no small thing. Around 40 percent of all first marriages in this country end in divorce, after an average duration of just eight years. Several of the couples we know—gay and straight—have divorced or parted ways in recent years. After a quarter-century with the same partner, I feel positively old-fashioned, like the lesbian Ozzie and Harriet. Many times, I wondered if we would make it this far. But we have, out of some combination of history and stubbornness and love. And even now, we discover each other.

"I dreamed you and Mommy got married again," Hannah says to me one day as I am driving her to school. "You wore sparkly gold dresses and gold shoes with straps and had roses."

"Maybe we'll have an anniversary party," I say to her.

"No," she says. "I want you to have another wedding. I want to be an attendant." Hannah's on a mission. "I have the bridesmaids' dresses all planned in my head," she adds. I have no doubt that she does. In Hannah's hands, a second wedding would have all the glamour the first one lacked. This time, the reception would not be in a church basement with one orange wall and a rented dance floor. There would be no do-it-yourself decorations. Hannah would have sparkle. Baskets of flower petals, an ice sculpture, a tiered cake, golden gowns. Lesbian moms, meet Barbie Wedding.

Hannah would like us to get married, preferably in a ceremony involving at least one stretch limo. But would we like to? In the years since we held our wholly ceremonial and legally irrelevant wedding, marriage has become a real possibility, at least in some states. Would we want to get married again, this time legally, in Canada or Massachusetts or Vermont or, now, Iowa?

Maybe, although at this point, it feels vaguely redundant. The legal recognition would be nice and even nicer if it actually applied in Minnesota. But what I do know is this: marriage or not, we are a family. We are part of one another.

Just before Hannah's sixth birthday, Jane and I sign up for a Committed Couples Class at the Unitarian Church we have begun to attend since leaving our suburban home and moving back to St. Paul about a year and a half ago. It's a seven-week course led by the senior ministers who have, not incidentally, been married to each other for thirty years. During the introductions, I look at the small stack of handouts we have been given and see that we will have homework every week. This pleases me; it's like having mandatory Big Issues to discuss. Our first assignment is to develop a Mutual Relationship Vision. I flip through the instructions, all seven pages of them. I love this stuff. It's like a women's magazine quiz on steroids. I wonder what Jane will think. "Oh, holy cats," she murmurs.

To figure out our Mutual Relationship Vision, we are supposed to write one-sentence, positive-language answers to a series of simple questions like, oh, "What do you feel toward each other?" and "What is your sex life like?" But here's the most important part: we are to write the sentences as if they are already true. This is to be our vision, even if it is not always our reality.

During the week, Jane and I each work on the homework separately, as the instructions say to do. Then, over dinner one night, we sit with Jane's laptop and type up a list of answers that merge her responses and mine. Some of the statements are easy. We both have written that we make each other laugh. That we talk through major decisions together. That Hannah is at the center of our world. But some of the statements are more complicated, carry more baggage, are harder won. I advocate for including a sentence about taking time apart to cultivate our own selves. And another about being able to express, and make room for, our own needs. Jane lobbies for: We accept each other and embrace our differences. These are some of the things that have bedeviled us the past few years. Truthfully, they were probably there all along, but they were not nearly as noticeable because the daily needs of a child were not present to pull them into focus.

A friend tells me that every person in a long-term relationship eventually discovers that they are no longer married to the person they fell in love with. This is true, I think, but only half true. After twenty-five years, Jane and I are no longer the same people—and we are exactly the same people. This is blessing and curse, on both sides of the equation. We each have changed in some ways; we each will never change in others. But I feel like we have come—and are coming—much closer to a place where these visions are, in fact, realities—not in spite of Hannah, but because of her.

One morning in the summer before Hannah started kindergarten, I walked with her out of the house on our way to the nearby park. The sun glowed in the bright blue sky; a light breeze blew on our faces. This is Minnesota at its best, our short, sweet summer radiant with light.

"It's another glorious day," I say to Hannah. "What will we do with all of these glorious days?"

"Put them in our pockets," she says, matter-of-factly. "Then, when we need one, we can take it out and throw it in the air."

Hannah stretches her arm as high as it will go, reaching for the sun. She touches the bluest blue sky. And she grabs it in her fist and quickly, quickly, sticks it in her pocket.

"Got it," she says. We do this all summer, whenever the day is especially beautiful. She catches the day, puts it in her pocket, and saves it.

And someday, when we need it, we'll take one out and throw it in the air.

Acknowledgments

Thank you to my editor, Gayatri Patnaik, for her enthusiastic commitment to bringing this book out into the world. Thank you to Jeremy Adam Smith for his commitment to paying it forward. Thank you to Elizabeth Wales and John Rosengren for their generous advice and support.

Many thanks to the writers and friends who responded to earlier versions of the text: Merie Kirby, Lee Thomas, Patrice Koelsch, Jon Spayde, Cris Anderson, Margaret Hasse, Marisha Chamberlain, Rita Benak, Carol Ann Larson, Hazel Lutz, Kathy Ogle, and Barb Vaughan. Thank you to Sasha Aslanian for helping me find the title.

Thank you to all the families with lesbian, gay, bisexual, and transgender parents who, in their everyday lives, are transforming what it means to be family.

Most important, thank you to Jane and to Hannah for being part of my life and allowing me to share a story that is as much theirs as it is mine.

Resources

The growth in the number of families with lesbian, gay, bisexual, and transgender (LGBT) parents has led to a corresponding growth in the number of formal and informal organizations that support our families. Among these are the following:

COLAGE
1550 Bryant Street, Suite 830
San Francisco, CA 94103
415-861-5437
www.colage.org

COLAGE is a support and advocacy organization for children of gay, lesbian, bisexual, and transgender parents. COLAGE has chapters all over the United States, as well as in Canada, England, and Sweden.

Family Equality Council
P.O. Box 206
Boston, MA 02133
617-502-8700
www.familyequality.org

Formed by a group of gay fathers in 1979, Family Equality Council supports and advocates for LGBT families and sponsors the annual Family Week in Provincetown, drawing some four hundred families. Family Equality Council also maintains an online list of support and social groups for LGBT parents across the country. Rainbow Families, based in St. Paul, Minnesota, serves LGBT families in the Upper Midwest and is now the Midwest office of the Family Equality Council.

GLSEN (Gay, Lesbian, and Straight Education Network)
90 Broad Street, 2nd Floor
New York, NY 10004
212-727-0135
www.glsen.org

With more than forty chapters nationwide, GLSEN works with educators, policymakers, community leaders, and students to address anti-LGBT behavior and bias in schools. GLSEN also offers resources and networking opportunities to school-based gay-straight alliances.

Human Rights Campaign
1640 Rhode Island Avenue NW
Washington, DC 20036
202-628-4160
www.hrc.org

The Human Rights Campaign is the nation's largest lesbian, gay, bisexual, and transgender civil rights organization. HRC offers extensive information online about the laws and policies that affect LGBT-headed families, including a guide to help adoption agencies become more open to LGBT parents.

Lambda Legal
120 Wall Street, Suite 1500
New York, NY 10005
212-809-8585
www.lambdalegal.org

Lambda Legal is a national organization that works to achieve full recognition of the civil rights of LGBT people and those with HIV. Based in New York, the organization has regional offices in Atlanta, Chicago, Dallas, and Los Angeles, and also has a national volunteer network of cooperating attorneys.

National Center for Lesbian Rights
870 Market Street, Suite 370
San Francisco, CA 94102
415-392-6257
www.nclrights.org

Through litigation, advocacy, and education, the National Center for Lesbian Rights works to advance the civil and human rights of LGBT people and their families. Its focus areas include families and parenting, marriage and relationship recognition, immigration, elder law, and transgender law.

National Gay and Lesbian Task Force
1325 Massachusetts Avenue NW, Suite 600
Washington, DC 20005
202-393-5177
www.thetaskforce.org

The National Gay and Lesbian Task Force works to develop the grassroots LGBT movement. The Task Force trains activists, and its Policy Institute provides research and policy analysis.

Our Family Coalition
870 Market Street, Suite 872
San Francisco, CA 94102
415-981-1960
www.ourfamily.org

Our Family Coalition offers educational programming, advocacy training, support, and social events to some 750 member families in the San Francisco Bay area.

Parents, Families and Friends of Lesbians and Gays (PFLAG)
1726 M Street NW, Suite 400
Washington, DC 20036
202-467-8180
www.pflag.org

PFLAG offers support and education to LGBT people, their families, and their friends. PFLAG also advocates for LGBT equality. The organization has more than five hundred chapters nationwide.

Printed in the United States
by Baker & Taylor Publisher Services